SCHLOSS

THE FASCINATING ROYAL HISTORY OF 25 GERMAN CASTLES

SUSAN SYMONS

Published by Roseland Books
The Old Rectory, St Just-in-Roseland, Cornwall, TR2 5JD
First published in 2014. This (second) edition published in 2016.

ISBN: 978-0-9928014-2-7
ISBN: 0-9928014-2-7

For my husband, Terry, with thanks for 25 years of fun, including our wonderful schloss tours.

CONTENTS

1

INTRODUCTION

For anyone interested in royal history, Germany is a treasure trove. The country was not fully unified until 1870, and before that there were lots of different duchies and principalities, each with its own reigning family. These have left their mark, not least in the hundreds of castles and palaces that dot the countryside.

Schloss is the German word for castle or palace and the pural is *Schlösser*. I started to write about these after my husband and I went to Germany in May 2013. Over three weeks, we drove through Lower Saxony, Mecklenburg-Pomerania, Berlin, Brandenburg, Saxony, and Hesse. We saw some very beautiful countryside, and it turned out to be a good time to visit; after an exceptionally cold and wet start to spring, the weather turned suddenly warm and dry. The trees came into leaf and were covered with blossom. There were fields of golden rape, lilac everywhere, and miles and miles of apple orchards.

In each area where we stayed, we decided to visit some of the many schlösser within easy reach. Over the three weeks, we saw 25 in all. These visits proved to be thoroughly enjoyable and quite fascinating. We learnt something about the history of each schloss and the family that had lived there, including some riveting personal stories. And we were also able to see how the fortunes of these wonderful buildings have varied over time, including the impact of the communist period on those that had been in East Germany (German Democratic Republic).

What is a Schloss?

In this book I have used the German word 'schloss' to denote a castle, palace, or stately home that once belonged to any of Germany's historical royal families. A more precise translation of the word schloss into English would be 'castle'. The schlösser I have included in the book range in time from fortified castles of the middle ages, such as Colditz or Stolpen; to grand palaces built in the 18th century in imitation of Louis XIV's Versailles, like Ludwigslust; to stately homes from the turn of the 20th century, such as Friedrichshof. The latest schloss to be built which I have included is Cecilienhof in Potsdam. This was constructed as World War I raged and was the last royal German schloss.

We visited some schlösser in good repair and others that were not, some that were clearly well visited and others where we were the only visitors in sight. We found many charming and helpful museum attendants who were delighted that we showed interest and asked questions but also encountered others whose purpose seemed to be continually to check tickets and permits and tell visitors what they could not do. And we found a huge variation in the quality and interest of the information on display at each schloss, as well as the accessibility of this to an English visitor.

What follows is a write-up of our visits and what interested us about the geography, history, or architecture of each schloss. It also tells some colourful stories of the historical royal characters associated with them. The book is set out on a geographic basis, with a chapter on schlösser in each of the modern-day German states of Lower Saxony, Mecklenburg-Pomerania, Berlin and Brandenburg, Saxony, and Hesse. At the back of the book there is a map of Germany, showing these states and the location of the schlösser.

This book is written very much from a personal perspective and does not attempt to be comprehensive. It is not an academic study but is intended to be an entertaining read from an author wanting to share her view that the history of royalty (the celebrities of their day) is fascinating and fun. Royal history is chock-a-block with drama, intrigue, and compelling personal stories, rather like a historical version of *Hello* magazine.

The history of Germany can sometimes seem confusing, and it is important to remember that, before 1870, it was not a single country. In the 1600s, there were hundreds of independent states, varying in size and importance and each with its own ruler and royal family. Over the following 250 years the number of these states would reduce, as they were amalgamated or annexed, particularly in the early 1800s after the French Revolutionary Wars and as a result of Bismarck's wars in the 1860s. Germany was eventually unified, under a German kaiser, or emperor, after the Franco-Prussian War of 1870.

The large number of independent states was the reason why Germany was the royal marriage market. There were more princesses of royal blood to choose from than in any other territory. A state might be poor and tiny, but the ruling family was considered to be of equal birth, and its daughters were therefore eligible. Since some of the states were Protestant and others were Catholic, the German marriage market was able to supply both Protestant monarchies, such as Great Britain and Prussia, and Catholic monarchies, such as Austria.

The hereditary titles of the ruling princes of these independent states can also be confusing, as they varied according to the size and importance of the principality. As well as king (könig), titles include duke (herzog) and the lessor ranking landgrave (landgraf) or margrave (margraf), both of which are a superior type of count (graf). In the 1600s all the rulers owed titular allegiance to the Holy Roman emperor, and at the top of the rankings were the seven electors (kurfürst), who were rulers of the most important German states and were responsible for electing the emperor. A further complication is that rulers often had the same first name, with names such as Georg, Friedrich, and Wilhelm being popular.

To assist the reader with these complexities, I have included what I hope are three useful appendices at the back of this book. The first has some brief information on the different royal families and main historical characters whose personal stories are included in the book. The second has simplified genealogical trees for some of these (these do not include all family members). The third appendix is a brief timeline to help readers connect the characters across time and country borders.

This is the second edition of this book. As well as revisions to the text, it has an improved layout, more illustrations, and updated information about the schlösser in the appendices.

I hope you will enjoy this book if you like royal history or old buildings or are simply visiting Germany and want to do some sightseeing. My husband and I have definitely discovered that visiting German schlösser is fun! We have already enjoyed more schloss tours and my second book on German schlösser has been published. So look out for *Schloss II: More Fascinating Royal History of German Castles.*

2

LOWER SAXONY AND THE HOUSE OF BRUNSWICK

We started our schloss tour in the state of Lower Saxony, in northwest Germany, where we stayed in the attractive little town of Celle. Lower Saxony (or Niedersachsen in German) is one of the largest of the 16 German länder, or federal states; in the north it borders the North Sea and in the west the Netherlands. Much of the present-day state was historically part of the kingdom of Hannover or the duchy of Brunswick, both of which were ruled by different branches of the Brunswick family and played an important part in European history.

The Brunswick family had many colourful members and we came across some fascinating stories as we visited their schlösser. These included the brothers who were at odds with each other over the family inheritance, a princess imprisoned for illicit love, and a king who lost his throne. (For a brief summary of the history of the Brunswick family, see appendix A on the royal families and main historical characters.)

Celle

1. Celle Castle with the unusual gable frontage.

Celle has a charming old town centre with many half-timbered houses, some dating back nearly 500 years. Our hotel, called the Füerstenhof, (or Princes Court) was close to the old town and the castle, in the former mansion of a courtier. We were in Celle on May Day, when the town was in holiday mode with live music and stalls of food and drink in the streets.

Celle Castle stands on a grassy mound next to the old town, surrounded by a moat and well-maintained gardens. It has a distinctive frontage, painted brown and white, with an unusual row of gables under the roof line. Celle Castle turned out to be a wonderful choice for our first schloss visit. It has an important role in the story of how a German duke came to be king of England, and the family drama and machinations that were played out here can match anything in *Hello* magazine.

We thought the curators at Celle Castle had done an excellent job in displaying the internal contents and telling the story of the castle and the inhabitants. They set a high standard against which we measured the schlösser to come. The information was set out in a way that was easy to follow, with lots of charts and pictures, and held the visitor's attention. The museum attendant in the ticket office was extremely helpful in answering questions and digging out a family tree from their files. Although there was no information booklet in English available in the ticket office or to buy in the bookshop, there was some English translation on the main exhibits. With the help of my husband's rusty A-level German from 50 years ago, we were able to unravel the fascinating story of the four dukes of Brunswick-Lüneburg and their women.

The four dukes were brothers, born in the 1620s, the sons of reigning Duke Georg of Calenberg and members of the extended Guelph family. Calenberg was just one of the many small states that then covered the territory that today is modern Germany. Georg of Calenberg is known as the Marrying Duke because he drew lots with his five brothers to decide which one of them would marry and carry on the line (Georg was the winner). The 17th century was a time when younger sons were both a necessity to ensure continuance of the family line, given the high rate of child mortality, but also a problem due to the understandable reluctance to split the family inheritance. Many became professional soldiers to earn their living, remained unmarried, and often died young in battle. In the case of Georg's sons, it was the youngest of the four, Ernst August, who had the most spectacular rise in the world, becoming an elector of the Holy Roman Empire and the ancestor of the kings of Denmark, Great Britain, Hannover, and Prussia. (See family tree 1 in the appendix of family trees for the four dukes of Brunswick-Lüneburg and the succession to the throne of Great Britain.)

The father of the four dukes, Georg of Calenberg, died in 1641, and his duchy of Calenberg passed to his eldest son, Christian Ludwig. However, a few years later, in 1648, Christian Ludwig was also in line for the duchy of Lüneburg. Under a family agreement, two sons in each generation would each inherit one of these duchies, and the two could not be held in the same hands, so Christian had to make a choice. He chose Lüneburg, with the seat of government in Celle because it was the economically stronger of the two duchies. Calenberg, with the seat of government in Hannover city, passed to his brother, Georg Wilhelm. This situation repeated itself in 1665, when Christian Ludwig died without heirs. Lüneburg with Celle Castle passed from him to Georg Wilhelm, and a third brother, Johann Friedrich, took Calenberg.

Georg Wilhelm undertook major works to transform Celle from a medieval fortress into a four-wing baroque royal residence complete with an enfilade of staterooms, which we can see today. Here he held his court, modelled on the French court at Versailles. Under Georg Wilhelm, Celle had a golden age.

So, the two duchies of Calenberg and Lüneburg had now provided for three of the four brothers. But the situation of the youngest brother, Ernst August, was still insecure, and there was tension over this, particularly between him and his brother Georg Wilhelm. This stemmed from an inheritance agreement the two had entered into.

Some years before, Georg Wilhelm had decided to marry and became engaged to Princess Sophia of the Palatine (another independent German state). For some reason, Georg Wilhelm later had cold feet and wanted to back out but without dishonour. Ernst August agreed to take over his brother's fiancé, and Georg Wilhelm agreed never to marry and to bequeath his duchy to Ernst August and his heirs.

Ernst August and Sophia were married in 1658 and, despite this inauspicious start and his open infidelity, had quite a successful marriage. They also secured a glittering inheritance for their children when Ernst August became elector of Hannover in 1692 and, after his death, Sophia was confirmed as heir to the throne of Great Britain. However, in the 1660s, all this was unforeseen and in the future, and Ernst August and Sophia were relying on their inheritance from Georg Wilhelm. The problem was that it looked as though Georg might not keep his word because he had met a woman.

2. Duke Georg Wilhelm of Celle and his duchess, Eleonore d'Olbreuse; their romance caused uproar in the family.

Georg Wilhelm fell in love with a French noblewoman called Eleonore d'Olbreuse. Although Eleonore was an aristocrat, she was not considered to be of equal birth, and the family must have assumed that she would become Georg Wilhelm's mistress[1]. But the commitment between the couple went deeper than this. They married unofficially in 1665 (called a marriage of conscience) and officially in 1676, although the marriage was not recognised by the family, and Eleonore was not accepted by them as duchess of Celle until 1680.

The relationship caused tension between the brothers and considerable worry to Ernst August and his wife Sophia. Their concern was that should Eleonore have a son, Georg Wilhelm would try to break the family agreement and leave his duchy to his son, rather than to his brother. Eleonore had a daughter, Sophie Dorothee, in 1666, and there were other pregnancies, although none of the other babies survived. But it was always possible that she could become pregnant again...

The tension did not ease until the death of the third brother, Johann Friedrich, in 1679 without male heirs. The duchy of Calenberg then passed on to Ernst August so that, at last, he became secure. The family agreement was renewed in 1680, when in return for Ernst August recognising Eleonore, Georg Wilhelm confirmed that Ernst August and his heirs would inherit the duchy of Lüneburg. And the problem was finally resolved in 1682 with the marriage of Georg Wilhelm's only child, Sophie Dorothee, to Ernst August's eldest son, Georg Ludwig, the future George I of Great Britain.

After the death of Georg Wilhelm in 1705, Celle Castle was occupied only from time to time, and as a result the town fell in importance compared to Hannover. Ernst August broke with family tradition and chose to combine the two duchies of Calenberg and Lüneburg rather than keep them separate, leaving his rights to both to his eldest son. This naturally caused strife with some of his younger sons and fractured the family. However, the combined wealth and power of both duchies enabled him to achieve his goal of being appointed elector by the Holy Roman emperor. Ernst August and Sophia became elector and electress of Hannover in 1692. Their son, Georg Ludwig, succeeded his father as elector and also became King George I of Great Britain after the death of Queen Anne in 1714. Hannover itself would become a kingdom in 1814.

In 1772, Celle Castle was refurbished as a refuge for a princess with a tragic fate. Princess Caroline Mathilde of Great Britain was the youngest sister of George III and born in 1751. After he became king, her brother arranged for her to marry her teenaged first cousin, King Christian of Denmark and Norway (his mother and her father were brother and sister). In 1766, at age 15, she was married by proxy in London, with another brother standing in for the bridegroom. Caroline Mathilde did not want to leave her family and her country for a husband she had never met and a country she did not know. She was in a flood of tears at her wedding and again the following day when she left for Denmark. But she had no choice. Although romantic love was recognised in the 18th century, and many girls did have a say in who they married, this was not the case for royal princesses. Their marriages were considered matters of state and arranged to further dynastic interests. Caroline Mathilde was not even allowed to take any English attendants to Denmark with her.

What Was the Holy Roman Empire?

The Holy Roman Empire of the German Nation was a loose alliance of the hundreds of independent German and central European states (principalities, duchies, and free cities) under the leadership of an elected emperor. By its name it claimed to be the successor of the Roman empire of the West, which fell to the Barbarians in the fifth century AD. The Holy Roman Empire existed for nearly a thousand years until it was disbanded in 1806.

The Holy Roman Empire was decentralised, which made it cumbersome and difficult to govern. Over the centuries, successive emperors were forced to grant concessions to the member states. These became increasingly autonomous, which weakened the central powers of the empire, so that the emperor's position became largely titular.

The Holy Roman emperor was elected by a college of kurfürsten or prince electors. The position of kurfürst was extremely prestigious and lucrative, second only in status to that of the emperor. In 1692, when Duke Ernst August was appointed elector of Hannover, there were only eight existing electors. These were the archbishops of Cologne, Mainz, and Trier and the secular rulers of Bavaria, Bohemia, Brandenburg, Saxony, and the Palatine. Over time, however, the election also became a formality, and the position of emperor became a sinecure of the Austrian house of Hapsburg, the male head of which was inevitably elected.

The rise of Napoleon and the French Revolutionary Wars led to the demise of the Holy Roman Empire. Following the annexation by France of German lands to the west of the Rhine and the defeat of Prussia and her allies at the battles of Jena-Auerstadt, a number of states left the empire to form the Confederation of the Rhine under Napoleon's leadership. Recognising that it had become untenable the last Holy Roman emperor, Francis II, abdicated and dissolved the empire in 1806. Thereafter he was Emperor Francis I of the Austrian empire.

By age 19, she was the mother of two children, Crown Prince Frederick and Princess Louise. However, the marriage was not a happy one. King Christian was mentally unbalanced and even before the wedding had earned a reputation for violence and immorality. Denied a fulfilling relationship with her husband, Caroline Mathilde fell head over heels in love with his doctor. Johann Struensee was a German who had an amazing career at the Danish court. After his appointment as court doctor, he soon became the confidant of the king. After a palace coup, during which he persuaded the king to abolish the council of ministers, Struensee became first minister of Denmark and Norway with almost dictatorial powers. He was also the lover of the queen and probably the father of her daughter, Louise[2].

Caroline Mathilde's happy idyll did not last long. In a counter coup led by the king's stepmother, she and her lover were arrested. She was charged with adultery and he with treason. Caroline Mathilde was imprisoned in Hamlet's castle at Elsinore, north of Copenhagen. She was allowed to take her six-month-old daughter with her but was separated from her son, who was heir to the throne. Here she was kept incommunicado, pending her trial.

Caroline Mathilde was found guilty and divorced from the king. Her lover, Struensee, was executed. There were plans to send her further away from court to the north of the country, but her brother came to her rescue. George III sent a convoy of British ships to Elsinore to escort her into a dignified exile. Because of the scandal she could not return to her childhood home; instead she was given refuge at Celle, in her brother's other kingdom of Hannover. This time she had to leave her daughter behind, as well.

Caroline Mathilde arrived in Celle as a virtual prisoner in 1772, when she was 21 years old. She never accepted that she was no longer queen of Denmark and never gave up hope of being reinstated and returning to her children. It was not to be. She died there from scarlet fever in 1775, aged 23.

Ahlden

Ahlden was the second schloss that we visited and was the prison of another tragic princess associated with Celle. Sophie Dorothee was the daughter of Georg Wilhelm and Eleonore and is known as the Princess of Celle. She was considered a beauty, and there is a charming portrait of her as a girl by Henri Gascar at the schloss, dressed as Flora, with flowers in her hair. The portrait included in this book, by Jacques Vaillant, is of a more mature woman with her children. She is dressed in fashionable and elegant clothes and adorned with expensive jewels. The portrait shows her beauty and style, inherited from her French mother.

3. Sophie Dorothee of Celle with her two children before her divorce.

As an only child, Sophie Dorothee must have been adored and spoilt by her parents, but her childhood came to an end at 16 in 1682 when she was married to her first cousin, Georg Ludwig, later George I of Great Britain. By 1687 the couple had two children, Georg August, the future George II of Great Britain, and Sophie Dorothee, a future queen of Prussia.

The marriage got off to a reasonable start, but the two were incompatible, and after a few years, it fell apart. Georg Ludwig started a long-term affair with one of his mother's ladies-in-waiting, Melusine von Schulenberg. Daughters were born to his mistress in 1692, 1693, and 1701. Meanwhile, Sophie Dorothee was unhappy, bored, and discontented. She probably knew about Georg's affair, although she may not have known about the children, who were passed off as nieces of his mistress. She began her own affair in secret with an army officer, Count Philipp von Königsmarck.

Their affair was passionate, but the couple were indiscreet and in many ways courted disaster. They ignored friendly warnings and continued to meet when they could, write to each other, and use intermediaries. Inevitably, their affair became known. In July 1694, Königsmarck left his lodgings in Hannover late at night for an assignation with Sophie Dorothee at the Leine Palace and was never seen again. The general view is that the gentlemen of the court did away with him on the orders of Ernst August and threw his body into the river[3]. Later that year, Sophie Dorothee and Georg Ludwig were divorced, and for her the terms were harsh. She was separated from her children and sent to the schloss at Ahlden.

Ahlden is privately owned, not open to the public and not in any of the guidebooks; we tracked it down ourselves on the Internet. This was our first brush with the problem that there does not seem to be any comprehensive list of schlösser in Germany, even those that can be visited. As our main reference, we used an excellent publication by Schnell and Steiner called *Time to Travel: Travel in Time*, but this does not cover all areas of Germany, and for the areas it does cover, it includes only those properties managed by the state heritage organisation. Much later on in our holiday, we also used another reference book that was kindly given to us by a museum attendant. This was *Schencks Castles & Gardens*.

4. Ahlden, where Sophie Dorothee of Celle spent over 30 years under house arrest.

The village of Ahlden is about 30 miles from Celle. It's a pretty place, but even today, it's something of a backwater. The schloss is small and probably better described as a manor house. It's currently in use as an auction house, but we were able to look at the outside. Sophie Dorothee was here under a form of house arrest for over 30 years, until her death in 1726. She was not allowed to see her children or to have any visitors other than her mother, and she could drive out only for a short distance. Over the years, her mother repeatedly lobbied for her daughter's release but to no effect. For a princess used to being the centre of attraction at the court at Celle, it must all have been very hard to bear.

Her divorced husband, Georg Ludwig, never married again. When he became king of Great Britain in 1714 and departed for his new country, he was accompanied by two female companions. In London they became known as the Maypole and the Elephant. The Maypole was his longstanding mistress, Melusine von Schulenberg, who was tall and thin. The Elephant, on the other hand, was short and fat. She was Sophia Charlotte von Kielmansegg, who at the time was also assumed to be his mistress; in fact she was his half sister, the illegitimate daughter of his father[4]. Both became naturalised Britons and were ennobled as the duchess of Munster and countess of Darlington, respectively. Georg Ludwig's relationship with his son, Georg August, never recovered from the sending away of his mother when he was a child. After they came to England the bitterness between the two men became an open breach.

Our visit to Ahlden gave food for thought. If Celle Castle and the story of the four dukes illustrated the problem of younger sons in the princely families of Germany, Ahlden brought home to us the sometimes tragic fate of their daughters in the lottery of arranged marriages.

Herrenhausen

Visiting Celle and Ahlden had told us the stories of Eleonore d'Olbreuse and her daughter, Sophie Dorothee. On the trail of Electress Sophia of Hannover, we went next to see the gardens at Herrenhausen.

Sophia was the wife of the youngest of the four dukes, Ernst August. She was more fortunate in her marriage than her daughter-in-law, Sophie Dorothee. Older and wiser at 28 when she married, perhaps she worked harder to make it a success and did not expect so much. Sophia is, of course, a very important figure in British history and was the founder of the Hanoverian dynasty. She has a fascinating life story. Born the child of an impoverished and exiled king and queen, she died aged 83 as the heiress to the throne of Great Britain. If she had lived eight weeks longer, she would have succeeded Queen Anne.

Sophia's father was Elector Friedrich V of the Palatine, an important state with lands straddling the Rhine. Her mother was Elizabeth Stuart, the daughter of King James I of Great Britain. Their marriage had great promise, but the couple's troubles began when rebels in Bohemia overthrew their king and started off the Thirty Years' War, which later engulfed much of Europe. The rebels offered the vacant throne to Friedrich, who took a gamble and accepted. In 1619 he moved his family to Prague.

His reign did not last long. After only one winter, Friedrich and Elizabeth were forced to flee Bohemia in 1620. They were unable to return home, as the Palatine had been invaded and was occupied by enemy troops. They lost everything and lived the rest of their lives in exile. They are known to history as The Winter King and Queen.

Sophia was their 12th child and was born in 1630, during their exile in Holland. Although of noble birth and well connected, she was entirely without fortune, and her prospects in life were not rosy. She counted

5. Sophia of Hannover in 1648.

herself lucky to receive an offer of marriage from Georg Wilhelm at what was then a late age of 28 and even made no objection when her fiancé backed out and passed her onto his brother, Ernst August. In 1680, when she was 50 years old, Sophia wrote her memoirs to amuse herself while her husband was away. Although written more than 230 years ago, her voice still comes through loud and clear. She tells us of the difficulties she faced living in her brother's house (he did not get on with his wife) and her desire for a home of her own. When her brother told her about the dukes' plan to pass her between them, she tells us that she replied,

> that a good establishment was all that I cared for, and that, if this was secured to me by the younger brother, the exchange would be a matter of indifference.[5]

However, the couple did fall in love after their marriage and delighted in each other's company. And although the duke's passion did not last forever, Sophia always remembered these happy times and learned to tolerate his affairs. After more than 20 years of marriage, Sophia would still write proudly of how much in love they had been as newlyweds and about their wedding night.

After her husband's death, Sophia's Stuart descent through her mother would bring her a great prize. By 1700 it was clear that Queen Anne of Great Britain would have no direct heir. Anne had a calamitous history of 17 pregnancies but no surviving children. Her last surviving child, the 11-year-old duke of Gloucester, died in 1700. It was imperative that an heir be found for the British throne and that the heir be Protestant.

Sophia had a claim, as she was the granddaughter of James I; also, she was well qualified, as she was a Protestant, and she had a son and grandson who could succeed her in due course. There were many other Stuart descendants who came before her in the order of succession, including the exiled James II and his son (the Old Pretender) and Sophia's own elder brothers and sisters. But none could offer these qualifications. Under the 1701 Act of Settlement, Sophia was confirmed as heiress to the throne of Great Britain. Queen Anne was 34 years younger than Sophia, but she was in poor health, and Sophia had every expectation of outliving her. She almost did. Sophia died on 8 June 1714, and Queen Anne on 1 August of the same year.

Herrenhausen gardens are Sophia's great achievement. The palace, on the outskirts of Hannover city, was the summer residence of the Hanoverian court. Their main residence and the seat of government was the Leine palace in the city centre. Sophia's brother-in-law, Johann Friedrich, was the builder of Herrenhausen Palace and first laid out the gardens. But the heyday of the palace began with Sophia and Ernst August, and it is Sophia who is most associated with the garden.

From 1680, when she first stayed in Herrenhausen, until her death over three decades later in 1714, Sophia worked to create the wonderful formal gardens at the palace. 'The garden is my life', she said[6]. She was inspired by the wonderful gardens in the palaces of the House of Orange in Holland, where she lived as a child. Under Ernst August and Sophia, Herrenhausen became the centre of an enlightened court admired across Europe and the meeting place for great names in European culture of the day, including the philosopher, Gottfried Wilhelm Leibniz, and the composer, Georg Friedrich Handel. When her husband died in 1698, he left the palace to Sophia, and it became even more important to her.

Aged over 80, Sophia would write:

> I must thank God for my good constitution, that I can still make the grand tour around the Herrenhausen garden without effort because I very much like to go walking in these beautiful pergolas.[7]

And she died in her beloved garden, suffering a heart attack while taking her usual afternoon walk and passing away before she could be moved indoors.

6. The garden of Sophia at Herrenhausen, with the new palace in the background.

The Right of Primogeniture

Primogeniture is the principle by which family property and titles are inherited by the eldest son, rather than being split between several heirs. This is to ensure that family wealth and rank are passed on intact without being diminished by division and redivision down the generations.

The principle of primogeniture was not always followed by the German royal families. In some families it was fortunately established early; for example, the Hohenzollern electors of Brandenburg followed primogeniture from 1473. In others the practice of division persisted much later; for example, when Duke Ernst I of Saxe-Gotha died in 1675 his lands were split between his seven sons, creating the separate but much smaller principalities of Saxe-Gotha-Altenburg, Saxe-Coburg, Saxe-Meiningen, Saxe-Saalfeld, and so on. The transition from one practice to another could be painful. When in the 1680s Duke Ernst August of Hannover decided to break with his family tradition and introduce primogeniture it caused great bitterness among his sons and fractured the family.

In later centuries primogeniture became the usual rule.

The palace of Herrenhausen was destroyed by an air raid during World War II (despite a request from the British royal family that it be spared), but the gardens survived and are still open to the public today. The Great Garden (Grosser Garten) is truly breathtaking, a huge rectangle set out in formal, intricate, colourful planting and bordered by an artificial canal and avenues of trees. The gardens are beautifully maintained, and on the day we were there, we saw an army of gardeners weeding. It was a lovely, warm, sunny day, and we wandered through the gardens enjoying the fruits of the gardeners' hard work and the wonderful spring flowers.

To my mind, a garden is always best seen as an adjunct to the house or palace for which it was designed. With the palace destroyed, the gardens at Herrenhausen have been rather 'stranded' and without a focal point since World War II. However, the good news is that this is no longer the case, as the palace has been rebuilt, funded by the Volkswagen Foundation. The builders were still finishing off the palace, which was due to open later in the month, when we were there in early May 2013. The exterior of the new palace is a replica of the old, but the interiors are modern in design and will provide museum and function space.

In June 2014 the new palace at Herrenhausen was the venue for the official birthday party of Queen Elizabeth II, hosted by the British Ambassador to Berlin and attended by her son, Prince Andrew. It is fitting that this party, which celebrated 300 years from the accession of the Hanoverians to the British throne, was held in the beloved home of the founder of the dynasty.

Marienburg

Our final schloss in Lower Saxony is also strongly associated with a female member of the ruling family. Schloss Marienburg is named after Queen Marie of Hannover. Her husband, King George V of Hannover, commissioned the building and gave it to her in 1858 as a 40th birthday present. The castle was still under construction in 1866, when Hannover sided with Austria and against Prussia in the Seven Weeks' War. Defeat was swift, and King George and Queen Marie lost their throne. Hannover was annexed and became a province of Prussia. Schloss Marienburg was never fully finished.

King George V of Hannover was the son of King Ernst August and his wife Friederike of Mecklenburg-Strelitz. He was one of a crop of royal babies born in spring 1819 as the result of what was called the Royal Race for the British Crown[8]. The race was triggered by the death in childbirth in November 1817 of Princess Charlotte of Great Britain. She was the only child of the Prince Regent (later George IV of Great Britain) and the only legitimate grandchild of his father, George III. Her death gave rise to the incredible situation that there was no heir to the British throne in the next generation (incredible because George III had 15 children).

7. The fairy-tale castle of Marienburg dominates the landscape.

So, after her death, Charlotte's middle-aged bachelor uncles, sons of George III, rushed around Europe trying to persuade eligible princesses to marry them and start the race to father the future king or queen of Great Britain. George of Hannover's parents had been married two years before, but they also took part in the race. Four babies were born between 26 March and 27 May 1819, only 18 months or less since Charlotte's death. George V of Hannover lost the race to his cousin, Victoria. She was born three days before he was, but more importantly, her father was the fourth son of George III, and his father was only the fifth. But had Victoria not survived to grow up and have children, King George V of Hannover would also have been king of Great Britain.

The kingdoms of Hannover and Great Britain were ruled in a personal union by the same monarch between 1714 (when the elector of

Hannover became George I) and 1837 (when Queen Victoria succeeded to the British throne). Under the laws of Hannover, a woman could not succeed to the throne if there was a male in the family, so the two kingdoms were again separated in 1837, and Victoria's uncle became King Ernst August I of Hannover instead of her. (See family tree 2 for the separation of the kingdoms of Hannover and Great Britain.) King Ernst August I of Hannover, however, also remained the next in line to Victoria. He was a hated figure in Britain, popularly suspected of heinous crimes, such as incest and murder.

In my personal collection of Victorian prints, I have a 'Spooner of London' print from the 1830s, called The Contrast. On the left it shows England, personified in the figure of a young, fresh, and pretty Victoria; on the right is Hannover in the figure of the elderly and unattractive King Ernst August. His unpopularity meant there was pressure for

8. The Contrast: print comparing the elderly King Ernst August of Hannover, with the young and popular Queen Victoria.

Victoria to marry as soon as possible and produce an heir. She married Prince Albert of Saxe-Coburg-Gotha in February 1840, and their first child, Victoria, Princess Royal, was born in November of the same year.

King George of Hannover was blind from childhood. He lost the sight of one eye very young from illness and the other from an accident a few years later. In all the portraits that we saw, he is shown in profile, never full face, partially to disguise his disability. In the entrance hall at Marienburg, there is a cork model of the castle that was made so he could form a picture of the castle by feeling the model.

As a child, King George was considered as a possible bridegroom for his cousin, Victoria, which might have again united the kingdoms of Great Britain and Hannover. However, his blindness was considered to disqualify him. He married Marie of Saxe-Altenburg, and the couple had three children. They built Marienburg as their summer residence and intended it to be an impressive castle and a symbol of the wealth and power of the Hanoverian royal family.

Built in imitation of a medieval castle and sited on a hilltop, it is a fairy-tale schloss visible from miles away and dominates the landscape. This was the time when gothic revival was all the fashion, and many castles were remodelled in this romantic image of the past. As the personal property of Queen Marie, it could not be expropriated when Hannover lost the war with Prussia in 1866 and King George lost his throne. It remains in the family ownership today. King George and his son, Crown Prince Ernst August II, were exiled, but Queen Marie and her daughters moved into Marienburg until they, too, were 'frozen out' by the new government in 1867 and joined King George in Gmunden in Austria. Since then, it has only been lived in for a few years, between 1945 and 1955, by the couple's grandson, Ernest August III, Duke of Brunswick, and his wife, Princess Viktoria Luise of Prussia (the only daughter of German Kaiser Wilhelm II).

The wedding of Ernst August III and Viktoria Luise in 1913 was the last great gathering of European royalty before the calamity of World War I that resulted in many of them losing their thrones. Their

HIS HIGHNESS PRINCE GEORGE-FREDERICK-ALEXANDER
CHARLES-ERNEST-AUGUSTUS OF CUMBERLAND

George

9. King George V of Hannover as a young man; he was always shown in
profile to help disguise his disability.

marriage helped to heal the bitter breach between their families,
started by Prussia's annexation of Hannover in 1866. Ernst August's
family finally renounced their rights to the Hanoverian throne, and in
return it was agreed that he could succeed to the duchy of Brunswick,
which had been under a regency since the senior line of the Brunswick
family died out in 1884.

In her memoirs published towards the end of her life, Duchess
Viktoria Luise wrote of the chaos in Germany at the end of World
War II and how she and her husband fled west to escape the Soviet
army to Marienburg in the British zone of occupation, saving what
possessions and family heirlooms they could. Initially only two rooms

were habitable, there was no electricity, and building materials for improvements were scarce. But they were happy to be in his ancestral home, and things gradually improved and got back to normal.

The duke died in 1953 and was laid in state in the great hall at Marienburg, clad in the black uniform of the famous regiment of Brunswick Hussars. The duchess's memoirs talk movingly about his funeral procession to the cathedral in Brunswick city. In accordance with his wishes, he was buried in the garden at Herrenhausen, having told his wife,

> I want to lie in God's beautiful scenery, where children can play around my grave.[9]

Close by in the Herrenhausen gardens is the mausoleum of his great-grandparents, King Ernst August I and Queen Friederike of Hannover. Also buried here are his earlier ancestors, Electress Sophia of Hannover and her son, George I of Great Britain.

Marienburg is built around a rectangular courtyard, with four wings, including a medieval keep, the castle chapel, and what looks like a gatehouse but in fact does not lead out of the castle. The interior, as well as the exterior, is in gothic revival style. The rooms must still look very much as they did when Queen Marie and her daughters, Princess Frederica and Princess Marie, were there, including Queen Marie's suite of rooms with its gorgeous circular library and her daughters' salon with a serene and cosy window corner with window seats. Also on display is a fabulous suite of silver furniture, dating from the 1720s and originally acquired during the time that Hannover and Great Britain were ruled together. Large silver objects were considered a status symbol for royal rulers.

Marienburg was the first of our schlösser that was busy with visitors. At Celle Castle, there was only a handful of other visitors, and at Ahlden, there were none. Herrenhausen gardens were clearly popular but are big enough to absorb large numbers of visitors, and we hardly bumped into anyone. Marienburg is relatively small and was full of visitors doing guided tours.

The schloss at Marienburg could be visited only by guided tour. These left regularly but were in German only, so we were tacked onto the end of one with an audio tape in English. We are always nervous about guided tours as they are so dependant on the knowledge and approach of the guide; they can be excellent or just a rehearsed patter. We prefer to move at our own pace, look selectively at what we find of interest and at any printed information in English, and ask questions. However, we can understand their attraction to control a large numbers of visitors in a small area, and where there is little else in English an audio guide is a real boon.

3

MECKLENBURG-POMERANIA AND THE MECKLENBURG ROYAL FAMILY

The next stop on our tour of schlösser was the state of Mecklenburg-Pomerania (or Mecklenburg-Vorpommern) in northeast Germany. Here, for the first time, we were in what used to be the German Democratic Republic (GDR), behind the Iron Curtain.

Mecklenburg-Pomerania is a very beautiful area of Germany and the least densely populated of the länder. It faces Denmark and Sweden across the Baltic Sea, borders Poland to the east, and includes many lakes and islands. The present-day state is made up of what were, until 1918, the independent principalities of Mecklenburg-Schwerin and Mecklenburg-Strelitz, (ruled by different branches of the Mecklenburg family) and also part of the Prussian province of Pomerania. (See the appendices for a brief history of the Mecklenburg family.)

The countryside was in the full flush of spring while we were there, and the Baltic Sea has a special serene, blue quality, fringed with beaches of white sand. Miles and miles of good roads in the area lined with newly planted trees spoke to major new investment in infrastructure, and we drove past acres of wind farms and solar panels. However, there were still signs of the ravages of the communist years, and not everywhere is sharing the benefits of the growing German economy. This would be illustrated in the schlösser that we saw.

Grand Duke's Palace, Bad Doberan

We stayed at the Grand Hotel Heiligendamm, a spa resort on the coast of the Baltic Sea (or Oostsee as it is called in Germany). The resort has royal connections, having been founded in 1793 by the ruling Duke Friedrich Franz I of Mecklenburg-Schwerin. Sea bathing had recently become fashionable across Europe due to its perceived medicinal benefits. Duke Friedrich Franz took his first sea bath here in 1793, on the advice of his doctor. Four years earlier, King George III of Great Britain had done the same at Weymouth on the south coast of England. George III's patronage and regular visits transformed

10. The elegant garden front of the Grand Duke's Palace in Bad Doberan.

Weymouth into a thriving tourist resort, graced by elegant Georgian architecture. Friedrich Franz did the same for Heiligendamm and the town of which it is part, Bad Doberan.

Following the duke's lead, fashionable society flocked to Heiligendamm to try out the benefits of sea water. This was the time of the invention of bathing machines and swimming costumes, some early examples of which can be seen in the Bad Doberan museum. Visitors would stay in Bad Doberan and drive out four miles to the coast for sea bathing each day. In 1796 there were the first building developments— the Bath House at Heiligendamm for sea water treatments and the Lodging House in Bad Doberan that was the first hotel on the Baltic Sea coast. It was also the first building around the Kamp.

The Kamp is a small triangular green in Bad Doberan that was the centre of fashionable life. The museum has several contemporary prints showing elegant ladies with parasols accompanied by smartly dressed gentlemen in top hats, strolling around the Kamp or driving around it in carriages. It is still well worth a stroll today as all the important buildings in Bad Doberan's history as an early tourist resort are located around it and there are helpful plaques on each with translation into English. They include the Salon, built in 1802 as a restaurant and dance hall, the Chinese-style White Pavilion built in the middle of the Kamp in 1810 for music and refreshments, and the Grand Duke's Palace.

Friedrich Franz I had succeeded his uncle as duke of Mecklenburg-Schwerin in 1785 and would be elevated from duke to grand duke at the Congress of Vienna at the end of the Napoleonic Wars in 1815. He was married to Luise of Saxe-Gotha-Altenburg, and they had six children. In 1806 he commissioned local architect and builder, Carl Theodore Severin, to build a summer residence in Bad Doberan for the family. Severin was responsible for many of the buildings at Heiligendamm and Bad Doberan. The Grand Duke's Palace is a long, low, two-story building in classical style with four tall columns supporting the entrance. It opens directly onto what is now a busy road that makes the frontage appear cramped. At the back, however, part of the schloss garden is still there, so that the garden front has more room to breathe, and it is still possible to get an idea of what the palace would have been like in its heyday. It is used as offices by the local council and sadly is not open for visitors.

At the other end of the Kamp is the Prinzenpalais (or Prince's Palace), which is now a hotel. This was also built by Severin and acquired from him by Friedrich Franz for his heir in 1822. The story goes that Severin built this as his own home but that he did too good a job, so that it was coveted by the grand duke. Severin went on to build himself another home ten years later, just across the street, called Gottesfrieden (or God's Peace). It looks very similar in style to the Prinzenpalais, but he must have learnt by experience since it is a lot smaller.

Whilst you are strolling around the Kamp, you will probably hear the whistle of steam and the clanging of level crossing gates as the Molli approaches. This little steam railway runs right through the centre of town and on to Heiligendamm. It was opened in 1886 to take visitors there for the bathing and was known as the 'Bathing Line'. It still runs a scheduled service today, as well as being a great tourist attraction.

With the patronage of the grand ducal family and the growing popularity of seaside holidays more buildings also sprang up at Heiligendamm. All painted white they gave the resort the name of the 'White City on the Baltic'. The resort was very popular with Europe's

11. Burg Hohenzollern in the royal sea bathing resort of Heiligendamm.

nobility up until World War I. Prominent guests at this time included German Kaiser Wilhelm II and also Tsar Nicholas II of Russia and his family during their summer holidays. After World War II, the buildings were used as a sanatorium and convalescent home, but since unification they have again become part of a seaside resort. The Grand Hotel uses several of the historical buildings, including the old Kurhaus (built in 1816 in the form of a roman temple and used then as now for dining and social events) and Burg Hohenzollern (a miniature gothic castle built in the 1840s as holiday apartments). A huge granite boulder sits outside the hotel, put there in 1843 to commemorate 50 years from the founding of the resort by Friedrich Franz I in 1793. It is good to know that 220 years on it is back in use as a resort and going strong.

Ludwigslust

Our next visit in Mecklenburg-Pomerania was to the palace at Ludwigslust. The palace began as a small hunting lodge for Duke Christian Ludwig II of Mecklenburg-Schwerin (1683-1756). It was his son and successor, however, Duke Friedrich II (1717-1785), who transformed the modest lodge into a magnificent baroque residence on the lines of Versailles. Duke Friedrich became known as Friedrich the Pious. He wanted a secluded residence away from the tumult of the world, where he could carry out his duties, live a devout life, and pursue his interest in music, arts, and science. So, he transferred his residence and the seat of government of his duchy from the capital, Schwerin, to Ludwigslust. The palace was in its heyday under Duke Friedrich and his nephew Friedrich Franz I (1756-1837), who succeeded him. Together they reigned for 81 years. (See family tree 3 for the dukes of Mecklenburg-Schwerin and the builders of Ludwigslust.)

The long decline of the palace started in 1837, when Friedrich Franz died and was succeeded by his grandson, Duke Paul Friedrich (1800-1842), who transferred his residence and seat of government back to Schwerin. Ludwigslust was reduced to a mere summer residence, and Schwerin again became the focal point. In 1879, as part of this, substantial parts of the ducal art collection were moved between the two. The last duke, Friedrich Franz IV (1882-1945), abdicated at the end of World War I. He lived in one wing of Ludwigslust until his death, and some rooms in another wing were open to the public.

At the end of World War II and during the Cold War years, the palace suffered great losses. In common with many other previous royal residences situated in the GDR, the museum closed, and the buildings were put to other uses. The contents were scattered, the interiors were damaged, and the buildings deteriorated. During our tour, we came across schlösser that had been used as factories, lunatic asylums, political prisons, refugee camps, old people's homes, and even a police academy. Very often these years were glossed over in the information for visitors. Ludwigslust was used as government offices until 1986, when it was given to the Schwerin State Museum Department. Renovation is underway slowly and in stages.

Ludwigslust is named after Duke Christian Ludwig, who first built the hunting lodge. Translated, the name means 'Ludwig's delight', and it was a delight for us. The palace and the town were built to a grand design, with a long avenue leading to the palace square. On one side of this is the palace with the lovely gardens behind and on the other a wonderful cascade with another avenue behind it leading to the magnificent palace church. From the moment that we drove up the long avenue and parked the car outside the palace entrance in the square (no car park here!), this was our favourite schloss of the entire holiday.

Ludwigslust has an air of faded grandeur. The entry avenue and the schlossplatz (palace square) are large and grand, but there are weeds growing up through the cobbles. The palace itself looks awkward in the square—there were intended to be wings on three sides, but only the main wing was ever built. The park was laid out to a grand design, but postwar buildings have encroached on it, and parts have gone wild. But everywhere there were signs of recovery—the renovated palace church is open for visitors, the golden hall is under restoration, and gardeners are at work in the park. For us it felt like the palace in *Sleeping Beauty* coming back to life.

There were very few other visitors the day we were there. We were able to wander round at will, and there was no mandatory guided tour. The museum attendants were all charming and helpful. When one

12. Our favourite schloss—the palace square at Ludwigslust.

realised we were English, the young man in the ticket office took some trouble to search out information in our language and run after us with it. When we got out a camera, an attendant gently pointed out that we should buy a permit to take photos and helpfully ran back to the ticket office for it, while another showed us how to switch off the flash (no flash permitted). This was the first time we had bumped into the requirement to buy a photo permit, and it proved to be generally the case in the old GDR. And not least, the schloss has a good coffee shop (always welcome) located in the unique ambiance of the old hunting hall.

Duke Friedrich the Pious was an eccentric character. His piety led him to ban the theatre and other pleasures, such as playing cards and dancing. This was to the chagrin of his wife, Duchess Luise Friederike, who absented herself for several months each year to enjoy these pleasures elsewhere. It also caused him to be frugal, which led to one of the curiosities of Ludwigslust: the so-called Ludwigslust carton, or papier-mâché. This is everywhere; everything and anything was made of it—mouldings, pillars, decoration, chandeliers, furniture, ornaments. Even the statues in the park were made of papier-mâché.

The German Royal Marriage Market

The choice of marriage partner for a German prince or princess was a matter of state and rarely of personal preference. In an age when diplomacy was carried out by monarchs personally, marriages within their families were arranged to cement diplomatic alliances, establish rights of inheritance, and protect the family bloodline. Marriages outside these guidelines were not tolerated. This was the reason why Frederick the Great's father famously refused to allow him to marry an English princess; it would upset the Austrian emperor, who was Prussia's main ally.

Arranged marriages were the case right up to the end of the German monarchy in 1918. It appears from the memoirs of Princess Cecilie of Mecklenburg-Schwerin that her engagement to the crown prince of Prussia in 1904 was arranged by their mothers, although Cecilie claims to have fallen obligingly in love on sight. Love matches were rare and could cause political problems. When the crown prince's sister, Viktoria Luise of Prussia, fell in love with the son of the ex-king of Hannover in 1912, it caused havoc. This was because of the enmity between their families following the Prussian annexation of Hannover in 1866. The couple persisted, however, and did marry.

With multiple royal families, Germany was the royal marriage market for Europe. When George III came to the British throne in 1760 and wanted to marry there was frenzied activity at his court to review the eligible German princesses, and a list was drawn up. All of the Hanoverian kings of Britain were married to a German princess.

With both Protestant and Catholic states, Germany could supply princesses to both the Protestant monarchies of North Europe, such as Denmark and Britain, and the Catholic monarchies of further south, such as Austria. Most princesses were flexible about their faith when it came to a grand match. All of the tsars of Russia after Catherine the Great married German princesses, and all of them changed their religion to be Russian Orthodox. Germany could similarly supply princes for Europe's reigning queens. Queen Victoria married her cousin, Prince Albert of Saxe-Coburg. Another cousin, from the catholic branch of the Saxe-Coburg family, married the queen of Portugal.

It proved very successful as a cheaper alternative to traditional materials, such as wood and stone, so the factory at Ludwigslust went into commercial production and became a local industry. The exact details of the formula were kept secret, and Duke Friedrich supported the industry by ordering that all state offices provide it with their wastepaper. The business flourished for many years but went into decline in the 1820s as tastes changed, and the factory finally closed in 1835. It is now the Ludwigslust town hall.

Another delight for us inside the palace was the collection of family portraits from the 1760s and 1770s by the Mecklenburg court painter, Georg David Matthieu. They show the dress and jewellery of the sitters in great detail. They also include some surprising life-size, cutout, freestanding portraits—for example, of Princess Sophie Friederike as a child. She was the sister of Friedrich Franz I and later married Crown Prince Frederick of Denmark. The purpose of these cutout portraits is a mystery, but one idea is that they were fire screens[10].

One of the portraits by Matthieu was of a Mecklenburg princess who would be a winner in the lottery of arranged marriage. Princess Sophie Charlotte was the younger daughter of a younger son of the ruler of the tiny state of Mecklenburg-Strelitz, which was a separate line of the family. The size and population of Mecklenburg-Strelitz was only around a fifth of that of Mecklenburg-Schwerin; in 1871 it had a population of just 97,000. As a junior member of a minor and relatively poor principality, she might have been considered an outsider in the marriage stakes, but she was in the right place at the right time to become one of the most powerful women in the world. In 1761 she married King George III of Great Britain.

When the young king succeeded to the British throne in October 1760, he was in a hurry to get married. Sophie Charlotte's family had links with the British throne and supported Hanoverian policy in Germany. As a child her father had been a ward of the elector of Hannover before he became George I of Great Britain. Sponsored by the minister of Hannover, the 17-year-old Sophie Charlotte was selected by the king. They were married at St James's Palace, London, on 8 September 1761, on the same day they met.

The marriage was a meteoric stroke of luck for the house of Mecklenburg-Strelitz. It enabled Queen Charlotte's brother, Prince Karl, to obtain the lucrative post of governor of Hannover on behalf of his brother-in-law, and it must have been a factor in a later grand marriage in the family—that of Charlotte's niece, Princess Luise of Mecklenburg-Strelitz, to the crown prince of Prussia. The king of Prussia (the father of the crown prince) considered that although her family were poor, they were well connected[11]. Luise became the best-loved queen of Prussia, and we would come across her and her sister, Friederike, later in our tour. (See family tree 4 for the line of Mecklenburg-Strelitz and their royal brides.)

King George III and Queen Charlotte proved a devoted and faithful couple. He never took a mistress, and she more than fulfilled her dynastic obligations, giving birth to nine sons (three of whom became Kings—George IV and William IV of Great Britain and Ireland, and Ernst August of Hannover) and six daughters. However, King George suffered from bouts of illness, and in later years this overshadowed their lives, and they became estranged. Queen Charlotte became unhappy and lonely. She had a bad relationship with her grown-up children and behaved as practically a prison wardress to her spinster daughters, who lived in what they called the 'nunnery'. Later in our holiday, we would also meet one of her daughters, Princess Elizabeth, who did not escape the nunnery until she married at the late age of 47.

After looking at the inside of the schloss at Ludwigslust, we enjoyed walking round the gardens and watching the gardeners as they rhythmically raked the wide gravel paths in a line. We searched for the mausoleum of Helena Paulowna and found it difficult to locate at first, as the plan of the garden was a little confusing. Little Helena Paulowna was the second of the six daughters of Tsar Paul I of Russia and his wife, Tsarina Marie Feodorovna. Named by her grandmother, Catherine the Great, after Helen of Troy, she apparently grew up to be a beauty.

13. The mausoleum of Duchess Helena Paulowna, who died before she was out of her teens.

From birth, Helena and her sisters, like all royal princesses of the time, were destined to further state interests by arranged marriages to foreign princes. So, in 1799, at age 14, Helena was married to Prince Friedrich Ludwig of Mecklenburg-Schwerin, the son and heir of reigning Duke Friedrich Franz I, and came to Ludwigslust as a bride. The couple had a son, Paul Friedrich, in 1800 and a daughter, Marie Louise, three years later. But Helena Paulowna had only a very short life. She suffered from consumption, and just a few months after the birth of her daughter, in September 1803, she died.

Helena was a contemporary and friend of Queen Luise of Prussia. Both died young, but years after their deaths, in 1822, Helena's son, Paul Friedrich, married Luise's daughter, Alexandrine. Helena's widower, Prince Friedrich Ludwig, went on to marry twice more after her death, but he died in his forties and never became the reigning duke. So, Helena's son, Paul Friedrich, succeeded his grandfather, Duke Friedrich Franz I, in 1837. Helena is remembered in the lovely mausoleum at Ludwigslust, a small building with a pretty Palladian portico, where her husband and several other members of the Mecklenburg-Schwerin dynasty were also later buried.

And finally at Ludwigslust, we walked across the schlossplatz, past the cascade and down the avenue to the palace church. From the outside, this looks more like a Greek temple than a church, and the inside is astonishing!

Behind the altar rises an enormous painting, 14 metres high and covering 350 square metres. Painted (of course) on papier-mâché, it took over 30 years to complete and shows the announcement of the birth of Christ to the shepherds. The organ is behind the painting, which has been cunningly cut through to show the organ pipes as part

14. Statue of Friedrich Franz I outside the schloss at Ludwigslust.

of the design. At the other end of the nave is the duke's pew, which takes up the entire wall and has three levels: ground level for the duke, above him for ladies-in-waiting, and above that for the gentlemen at court. It looks more like the royal box at a theatre than a place for worship. For a duke who has gone down in history as Friedrich the Pious, the church is incredibly flamboyant.

Duke Friedrich II was buried in the granite sarcophagus in the middle of the nave. Ground out from a large boulder found nearby, it took 24 horses two days to drag it to the grinding mill.

Schwerin

15. Schloss Schwerin has an amazing position on an island in the lake in the centre of town.

We also went to the state capital, Schwerin, to see Schloss Schwerin, the largest schloss in the state of Mecklenburg-Pomerania. This has an amazing position on an island in the lake in the centre of town and surrounded by formal gardens. As we drove towards it, the gardens and the lake provided a wonderful backdrop to the palace, which looked very grand and imposing. We crossed the bridge to the island on foot to enter the palace under the statue of Niklot, who was the founder of the Mecklenburg dynasty. Later we learnt that the current head of the house of Mecklenburg-Schwerin is Duchess Donata and that her son and heir is another Niklot.

Although still under restoration, Schwerin was by far the smartest schloss that we visited in Mecklenburg-Pomerania. The palace did experience a period of decline in the long years when the duke resided at Ludwigslust and was in a sorry state when the seat of government was transferred back in 1837. Duke Paul Friedrich (1800-1842) planned to build a new palace in the garden but died suddenly, hardly before it had begun. His son and successor, Friedrich Franz II (1823-1883), decided instead to redesign and reconstruct the existing palace along the lines of a Loire Chateau. This new palace was formally inaugurated in 1857.

In 1913, however, a devastating fire destroyed around one third of the palace. Restoration work began but was halted in 1918 when the duke abdicated. Like Ludwigslust, Schwerin became state property, and from the 1920s the staterooms were a museum open to the public. In the Cold War years, Schwerin was also put to other uses, including as a military hospital and a teacher training college. But it was good news for the schloss that Schwerin was confirmed as the state capital on unification and that in 1990 the schloss became the seat of the state parliament. It is now the centrepiece of a prosperous city.

Schloss Schwerin was the birthplace of a princess who was apparently destined to become queen of Prussia and empress of Germany. I say 'apparently' because the throne of Prussia toppled before she could become queen. Princess Cecilie of Mecklenburg-Schwerin married Crown Prince Wilhelm of Prussia, the son and heir of the last German kaiser, in 1905. Cecilie was born in 1886, the daughter of Duke Friedrich Franz III and his wife, Grand Duchess Anastasia of Russia, the cousin of Tsar Alexander III. Her marriage was the last occasion on which any German prince imposed a 'wedding tax' on his subjects; he did so to fund her dowry. During our schloss tour, we would also visit Gelbensande, where the couple became engaged, and Cecilienhof, the Potsdam palace built as their summer home.

As a child, Cecilie spent every winter away from Mecklenburg-Schwerin. Her father, Duke Friedrich Franz III, suffered from bad asthma and other complaints and needed a warmer climate in the winter. Each year, they stayed in Cannes from autumn until spring, and it was there that the duke died, aged 46, in 1897. In her memoirs

16. Crown Princess Cecilie and her two eldest children.

(published in 1931), Cecilie talked of coming home to Schloss Schwerin every May and about summer picnics in the grounds and outings on the lake with her sister, Alexandrine (who became queen of Denmark) and brother, Friedrich Franz (who was the last reigning duke of Mecklenburg-Schwerin). For them, the schloss was home, and the long absence every year only made their feelings more intense. She wrote:

> And although the castle no longer "belongs" to us since the revolution of 1918, my heart always beats more vigorously when I see it.[12]

Gustrow

After Schwerin, we went next to see the schloss at Güstrow. These two schlösser, at Schwerin and Güstrow, are connected by brothers and the story of sibling rivalry.

The practice of primogeniture (inheritance solely by the eldest son) was not established in all the German royal families in the 16th century. On the death of Duke Albrecht VII of Mecklenburg-Schwerin in 1547, there was a dispute between his sons over the inheritance. When this was eventually arbitrated in 1556, the lands were split. The eldest son, Johann Albrecht I, got the western lands and the castle of Schwerin, and the next brother, Ulrich, took the eastern lands with the castle of Güstrow. It was Johann Albrecht who undertook the extensive building work to transform Schwerin from a defensive castle into a princely residence; his brother, Ulrich, not to be outdone, did the same at Güstrow.

17. The schloss at Güstrow was remodelled by Duke Ulrich to rival his brother's at Schwerin.

As a result of his inheritance, Duke Ulrich was able to make a good marriage. In 1556 he married Elisabeth of Denmark, the daughter of King Frederik I. Her large dowry funded the building work at Güstrow. The couple had only one child—a daughter, Sophia, born in 1557, who married Frederik II of Denmark. When Ulrich died in 1603, he was succeeded by a younger brother, Karl, and eventually by a grandson of his older brother, Johann Albrecht I. The Mecklenburg-Güstrow line came to an end in 1695 with the death of the last duke, Gustav Adolf. After the death of the last duke's widow in 1719, the schloss at Güstrow reverted to the Mecklenburg-Schwerin line of the family. They used it as a secondary residence until the move to Ludwigslust. After that it was never used again as a residence and was left to fall into disrepair.

Time has been less kind to the schloss at Güstrow than to that at Schwerin. Despite this, it was our favourite of the two and felt much more personal than Schwerin. Duke Friedrich Franz I tried to demolish it but was opposed by the citizens of the town; in the event, one wing and the palace church had to be pulled down in the 1790s because they were unsafe. During the Napoleonic Wars, it was used as a supply depot and a field hospital and from 1817-1945 as a workhouse for social problem cases and political prisoners. Discipline was tough and conditions very poor. After the war, it housed refugees and was later used as an old people's home. Through the vicissitudes of these years, the contents were dissipated and the interiors completely altered. Post German reunification, it was renovated and became a museum with a large collection of religious art.

The schloss has a gaunt and forbidding aspect. As we passed the impressive gatehouse and crossed the old moat, it was easy to imagine the years when people were shut up there. It still feels like a neglected place. There were few visitors the morning we were there, and the schloss café advertised in the information booklet looked long since closed. But there was evidence of ongoing work—for example, to the gardens at the side of the schloss—and we felt that should we visit again in a few years' time, we would see further changes.

The lady in the ticket office was extremely nice to us, and when she heard of our interest presented us with a copy of *Schencks Castles and Gardens*[13]. When we left, she was helping a group of children, the only other visitors we saw, complete a project sheet. She recommended a coffee shop in the town just a few minutes' walk away, Café Küpper. This turned out to be one of the best we found on the holiday, with delicious homemade kuchen (cakes).

Jagdschloss Gelbensande

Further east along the Baltic coast, 25 miles from Bad Doberan and the other side of Rostock, is Jagdschloss (or Hunting Lodge) Gelbensande, where Crown Princess Cecilie became engaged. The schloss was built in the 1880s for Cecilie's parents, Friedrich Franz III and Anastasia, and was a favourite with all the family. They came here every summer, in time for her mother's birthday on 28 July and stayed on into the autumn. Cecilie devotes a whole chapter to Gelbensande in her memoirs, lovingly describing happy days on the beach, autumn rides through the woods, and stag hunting with her uncles from Russia.

Cecilie's mother was an interesting character. She was born Grand Duchess Anastasia Mikhailowna of Russia and was the daughter of Grand Duke Mikhail, the youngest child of Tsar Nicholas I. Anastasia (or Stassie as she was always called) was the only girl among six boys. Her brothers are said to have been devoted to her, which may have contributed to her becoming spoilt and self-centred. But she was married off young to Friedrich Franz III of Mecklenburg-Schwerin in a marriage arranged by her father, apparently without consulting her.

Stassie's father was the governor of the Caucasus, and she was brought up in Tiflis, far away from the Russian court in St. Petersburg. She found the Schwerin climate cold and damp and the court life stuffy. Her husband's ill health gave the couple a good reason to move abroad to a warmer, healthier climate for him, but naturally this was very unpopular with his subjects. Things gradually settled down into an arrangement whereby they spent a few months every year, from spring until autumn, in Mecklenburg and the rest of the time at their home in the south of France.

18. The neo-Gothic hunting lodge at Gelbensande where Cecilie became engaged.

The circumstances of Friedrich Franz's death in their Cannes home in spring 1897 are somewhat mysterious. He had been ill all winter, but his death seems to have been the result of an accident, or perhaps suicide. After his death Stassie rarely returned to Mecklenburg, and although she was still in her thirties she never remarried. Her independent lifestyle was considered scandalous, particularly when she gave birth to an illegitimate child a few years later. Because of this Kaiser Wilhelm II apparently banned her from visiting Berlin to see her daughter, Cecilie, after her marriage[14].

Such unpleasant facts are never mentioned in her daughter's memoirs. Cecilie puts a romantic glow over how, in September 1904,

Crown Prince Wilhelm proposed to her at Gelbensande. But it was hardly a surprise, and the whole thing had been carefully stage-managed. The first step, some months previously, had been a meeting and vetting for Cecilie with his parents, before she had even met the crown prince. This had been followed by a letter to her mother from the kaiser asking for Cecilie's hand for his son. There was little opportunity for courtship or dating among royal couples; Cecilie and Wilhelm had met only twice before he proposed. Her answer was a dead certainty and had already been relayed to Berlin.

As it was when Cecilie became engaged, Jagdschloss Gelbensande is still set in a clearing and surrounded by tall pines. We parked the car and walked up the narrow drive between the trees. The schloss when it came into view was almost a shock; nothing could be more in contrast to the classic white simplicity of the Grand Duke's Palace in Bad Doberan. Described as neo-Gothic cottage style, the jagdschloss is a riot of turrets, gables, dormers, and balconies in decorative brickwork

19. The museum and restaurant at Gelbensande.

and half timbering. Perhaps we should have been more prepared because we had already seen the school and museum built by the same architect in Bad Doberan, Gotthilf Ludwig Möckel. From Severin at the beginning of the 1800s to Möckel at the end, architectural taste certainly changed dramatically over the 19th century.

Gelbensande remained in the ownership of Cecilie's family until the end of World War II. In May 1945 it became a hospital after a train full of injured soldiers got stuck nearby. It remained a hospital or nursing home until the 1980s and was then used by the local council for a variety of things including a library and old people's home.

Today the jagdschloss is home to a museum run by its Society of Friends on the first floor, in the family's old rooms, and a restaurant on the ground floor. This was closed on the day we visited, and the schloss was deserted, just some children playing in the drive with their bicycles.

Inside the décor, in accordance with the tastes of the day, is dark and cluttered, with stained-glass windows and wood panelling. In the museum foyer is inscribed the Latin motto of the House of Mecklenburg—'Per aspera ad astra', which roughly translates as 'Through hardship to the stars'.

The schloss was built as a holiday home and not as a palace for state business, and the family's rooms are quite small. They hold a tantalising exhibition of portraits, photos, and other memorabilia of Friedrich Franz, Stassie, and their children and grandchildren. I found it tantalising because there was no translation, and the only thing in English was a short handout to borrow.

We chatted with the friendly museum attendant and between us translated what we could. The society has carried out a lot of restoration work, but funding is an issue. One room that has been beautifully restored, using Möckel's original drawings, is the grand duchess's dressing room. Here a wrought iron spiral staircase rises to a galleried landing around two walls, lined with wardrobes. This is where Stassie's maid kept her dresses.

Wiligrad

20. Wiligrad is now an artists' colony and sculpture park.

Our last schloss while staying in Heiligendamm was quite unusual. Wiligrad Palace was built between 1896 and 1898 by Johann Albrecht of Mecklenburg-Schwerin for his first wife, Elisabeth of Saxe-Weimar-Eisenach. It was the last royal schloss built in Mecklenburg. Johann Albrecht was the brother of the reigning Duke Friedrich Franz III and, after the duke's early death in 1897, the regent for his minor son, Friedrich Franz IV, born in 1882. Elisabeth died in 1908, and a year later, Johann Albrecht married a second wife, Elisabeth of Stolberg-Rossla. They continued to live there until his death in 1920, when the second Elisabeth and the family moved away.

Wiligrad is in a secluded lakeside location on the Schweriner See and was hard to find. The palace is set in a large park of over 200 hectares, surrounded by subsidiary buildings. The remote location is perhaps one reason why, for 40 years, until German reunification in 1990, it was used as some sort of police academy. The area was restricted and fenced off and the park disfigured with drill grounds and firing ranges, bunkers, barbed wire fences, and a watchtower. The buildings in the grounds looked in disrepair, but we saw a lot of work underway to renovate them and to eliminate traces of the police academy years.

Wiligrad is included in the Schnell and Steiner publication, but it is not a stately home museum. The palace is an artists' colony and art gallery and is also used as a wedding venue. The grounds are a sculpture park. There was an exhibition of drawings by the celebrated East German artist, Bernhard Heisig (1925-2011), in the palace when we were there. Heisig is a controversial figure because of his previous links with both the Nazi and the East German regimes.

However, we were welcomed when we turned up and were sold entry tickets, and someone who spoke a little English showed us round. The interiors still looked very much like some old photos on display from a hundred years ago but without the contents. There were no other visitors.

21. Wiligrad is surrounded by subsidiary buildings.

A Schloss Restored—Gamehl

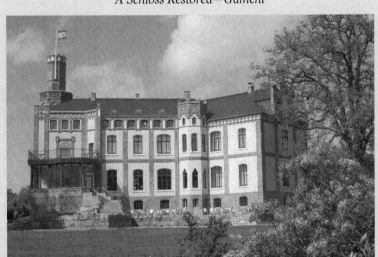

The garden front of Schloss Gamehl as it is today
(courtesy of Dagmar von Stralendorff-Wallis).

In 2001 Dagmar von Stralendorff-Wallis and her husband purchased Schloss Gamehl, just outside Wismar in Mecklenburg-Pomerania, at an auction. The Stralendorffs had been the owners of Gamehl for more than 550 years until it was expropriated by the Soviet occupying forces after the end of World War II. Her grandparents were forced to leave the schloss, and her grandfather, who was in his 80s, died just a few weeks later. Her father was a prisoner of war in Russia; he never saw Gamehl again.

The current schloss dates from the 1860s and was built by Dagmar's great-grandfather, Franz von Stralendorff, who was a senior official (chamberlain) at the court of the grand dukes of Mecklenburg-Schwerin. He demolished the previous building and built a new schloss in neo-Gothic style. He had more than 20 children from two marriages, but many had died as children. He wanted the new schloss to be a healthy home, so he built it facing south with large windows, a terrace, and a winter garden.

At the end of the war Gamehl was packed with refugees, mostly those fleeing westwards from the eastern parts of Germany. In the GDR years it became apartments for multiple families and also housed a kindergarten, grocery shop, and post office. Like so many schlösser in the old Eastern Germany it was poorly maintained and deteriorated. An old photo of the garden front from these years shows peeling paint and rising damp; the winter garden and terrace have disappeared and the garden is nonexistent. It is an amazing contrast to the schloss as it is today after restoration (see photo on the opposite page).

On the reunification of Germany in 1990, it was expected that expropriated property would be restored to the original owners. This did not

The schloss during the GDR years
(courtesy of Dagmar von Stralendorff-Wallis).

happen, and their only option was to buy it back. Dagmar and her husband tried to buy Gamehl in the 1990s but were not successful until the auction in 2001. They then faced huge problems with the restoration. These included not only first raising the finance, then gutting the building and eliminating rampant dry rot, but also how to restore it to keep the historic character of the schloss and make it commercially self-supporting. It all took several years, and Schloss Gamehl opened as a hotel in 2008.

The result of the work is a complete success. The schloss has been beautifully and faithfully restored. The exterior looks as it did before the deprivations of the GDR years and inside the light-filled rooms have striking décor and the most up-to-date comforts. There are still many schlösser in the old GDR in bad repair or struggling to find a use in the modern world. Schloss Gamehl is a great example of one that has been rescued and restored to glory.

For further information on Schloss Gamehl visit www.schloss-gamehl.de

SCHLOSS

4

BERLIN, BRANDENBURG, AND THE HOHENZOLLERNS

From Mecklenburg-Pomerania we drove south through the state of Brandenburg and what was once the heartland of imperial Germany. Brandenburg was just a frontier state of the Holy Roman Empire when it was purchased by the Hohenzollern family in the 15th century. During our stay here we would visit schlösser built by Hohenzollern princes, kings, and emperors, as this family rose from obscurity to preeminence among all the German royal families. (For a brief history of the Hohenzollerns, see appendix A.)

Our destination was the capital of Germany, Berlin. Although the city is surrounded by Brandenburg it is not part of that state and is one of the 16 German länder created on the reunification of West and East Germany in 1990. In Berlin we stayed on the Unter Den Linden in the old Eastern zone, near the Brandenburg Gate. For the generation to which my husband and I belong, brought up during the Cold War, the Brandenburg Gate was the symbol of the Iron Curtain, part of the Berlin Wall with barbed wire and border guards. So, it is amazing to see it today, restored to glory and with an open space used for 'happenings' in the same way as Trafalgar Square in London. We saw gymnasts making human towers, break-dancers being filmed, and lots of stretch limos with hen parties.

Altes Palais

The Unter Den Linden (or under the lime trees) was the ceremonial route for the Prussian monarchy, and it was through the Brandenburg Gate and down this route that Vicky drove on her ceremonial entry into Berlin in February 1858. She was Victoria, Princess Royal of Great Britain and Ireland, the eldest daughter of Queen Victoria, and she was 17 years old. She had been engaged since she was 14 to Prince Friedrich (Fritz) of Prussia, next heir after his father to the Prussian throne, and they had just been married in the Chapel Royal, London. It was a freezing cold day, and etiquette required that the ladies wear low-cut dresses. As she shivered in her coach, Vicky ordered the windows to be put down so the crowds could see her better.

Her destination was the Altes Palais (or old palace) on the Unter Den Linden, where she and Fritz were initially to live, and where King Friedrich Wilhelm IV and Queen Elisabeth were waiting to receive them. The queen asked,

> Are you not frozen to death?
> Yes, I am', replied Vicky. 'I have only one warm place and that is my heart![15]

Vicky came to Prussia with high hopes for the future. She was fortunate in her marriage, which would be a very happy one. But her dream of fulfilling her father's (Prince Albert) hopes of a unified Germany under a constitutional, liberal, Prussian monarchy would never be realised. Vicky and Fritz had to wait 30 years before he would succeed his father as Emperor Friedrich III, and by then, they were

22. Vicky at the time of her engagement to Prince Friedrich of Prussia.

already a footnote to history, and Prussia was an absolute monarchy, set on the militaristic path that led to World War I.

A ceremonial entry into Berlin was traditional for Hohenzollern brides. Over 60 years before, in December 1793, Queen Luise had made her entry to be married, and nearly 50 years later, on a blazing hot June day in 1905, in full evening dress and surrounded by red roses (her favourite flower), Crown Princess Cecilie came to be married to Crown Prince Wilhelm. The difference was that Vicky had been married in London, her parents having poured scorn on the idea of the Prussian royal family that the ceremony should take place in Berlin. Queen Victoria said she would not

> entertain the possibility of such a question as the Princess Royal's marriage taking place at Berlin...and the assumption of its being too much for a Prince Royal of Prussia to come over to marry the Princess Royal of Great Britain in England is too absurd, to say the least...Whatever may be the usual practice of Prussian Princes, it is not every day that one marries the eldest daughter of the Queen of England.[16]

As can be imagined, such high-handedness did not endear Vicky to her in-laws. She would always be an outsider to them, considered to be too English and not Prussian enough.

23. The Altes Palais in Berlin, where Vicky lived as a new bride.

Vicky and Fritz lived in the Altes Palais until their own palace nearby, the Kronprinzenpalais (Crown Prince's Palace) also on the Unter Den Linden, was ready for them. Before them, no one had lived in the Altes Palais for many years. Vicky found it antiquated, dark, cold, and dirty. She had been used to home comforts and the latest, up-to-date plumbing in her parents' homes. There were no bathrooms or toilets in the Altes Palais, and she had to walk through the death chamber of a previous king to reach her bedroom. It was a very cold winter, and despite fires everywhere, the palace was icy. Vicky developed a bad cough. In the spring, a large part of the ceiling in her sitting room fell down with a crash, close to where she was standing. It was a relief when they were able to move into their new home, in time for the birth of the first of their eight children. Prince Wilhelm of Prussia, later Kaiser Wilhelm II, was born in the Kronprinzenpalais on 27 January 1859.

It was a difficult and dangerous breach birth during which both mother and baby almost died. When William was born it was at first thought that he was dead, until he started to breathe. And sadly he was born with a damaged left arm that gave him a disability all his life. No one was sure how the damage was caused, but the arm never grew to the same size as the other and could not be used normally. As a child, William endured agonising and futile treatments to try to cure it, and as a grown-up he was at pains to try to disguise it. In portraits and photos he is often shown with his left hand in his pocket. It is interesting to speculate how much this disability contributed to his arrogant and pompous personality as an adult and how much blame for it contributed to his difficult relationship with his mother.

Both the Altes Palais and the Kronprinzenpalais were gutted during World War II. The buildings were rebuilt by the Soviet occupying powers in the 1960s, but the interiors did not survive. The Altes Palais is now part of Humboldt University, and the Kronprinzenpalais has been used for exhibitions and conferences. It was shrouded with scaffolding and under renovation when we were there, and it looked to be part of the development of the opera house (Staatsoper).

Sanssouci

24. Sanssouci was a favourite home of Frederick the Great.

On our first full day while staying in Berlin, we headed a few miles out of the city to Potsdam, the capital of the state of Brandenburg, where the Prussian royal family had their summer homes. We knew there would be a lot to see and that, as it was another public holiday, it would be busy. So, we arrived early, before opening time. But there was already a long queue for entry tickets to Schloss Sanssouci, and it was moving slowly. We discovered the reason for this when we reached the ticket desk. With lots of palaces in and around Potsdam open to the public, there is a complicated ticketing system involving a choice of single or multiple entry tickets. All this had to be explained to each customer, and that took time. We thought there must surely be an easier way. It didn't even save us time later, as we still had to queue up at the next palace to exchange our multiple-entry ticket.

Schloss Sanssouci is the oldest palace in the park. It was built in the 1740s by the most famous of Prussian Kings, Friedrich II, who has gone down in history as Old Fritz or Frederick the Great. He reigned for 46 years, from 1740 to 1786. When he came to the throne, he wanted a summer palace, where he could retreat from the ceremony and etiquette of court, along the same lines as the Grand Trianon at Versailles. He built a small, single-story building in rococo style, facing south on top of six curving terraces of vineyards and surrounded by large gardens.

It is a magical setting. The terraces of vines are still there in front of the palace, curving down the hillside to the Grand Fountain and the formal gardens below. Frederick was very proud of his vines, and they are still beautifully tended and trained in formal patterns along the terraces. We were intrigued by the mini greenhouses on the retaining wall of each terrace, where the vines are protected behind glass doors. It was a lovely, sunny day when we visited, and these doors were open. The yellow frontage of the schloss shone above them in the sun.

Frederick the Great was extremely fond of his summer rural retreat, and he called it Sanssouci, or Carefree. He came here to relax every summer that he could, from April until October, for the rest of his life. During the Seven Years' War he was away commanding the Prussian troops. On the eve of war he wrote a will, directing that if he died he should be buried in his garden at Sanssouci. And when the war was over, and Prussia had been victorious, he wrote to his brother Prince Henry that he had 'retired to his vine' at his favourite home[17].

There Frederick lived a celibate life with his invited, and exclusively male, guests. His wife, Queen Elizabeth Christine, was never invited. They were married when he was crown prince at the order of his father, who had selected her. Frederick never treated her as a wife, and his sexuality has been the subject of argument by historians ever since. The woman to whom Frederick was closest was not his wife or a mistress, but his sister, Wilhemine, who had shared his awful childhood. After he became king, he and his wife lived apart. The queen had her own palace at Schönhausen in the north of Berlin. They had no children, and Frederick was succeeded by his nephew.

At Sanssouci, the king read and played music and entertained his guests. He was a talented musician who played and composed for the flute. His flute playing contributed to the stooped posture that is so apparent in his portraits. Everywhere we went in Potsdam, there were reproductions for sale of the famous painting by Adolf von Menzel of Friedrich II playing the flute in a concert. The French writer and philosopher, Voltaire, was his guest at Sanssouci for some years, until the two had a falling out. In *Books and Characters: French & English* published in 1922, Lytton Strachey wrote about how the two might have spent their time there. During the day, Voltaire, 'a curious old gentleman, extremely thin, extremely active, and heavily bewigged'[18] worked away furiously at his writing. And in the evening there was music

> and the royal master poured out his skill in some long and elaborate cadenza, and the adagio came, the marvellous adagio, and the conqueror of Rossbach drew tears from the author of *Candide*.[19]

Frederick's decisive victory at the Battle of Rossbach in 1757, during the Seven Years' War, earned him the title of 'The Great'. *Candide* was Voltaire's most famous novel published in 1759. Frederick the Great died at Sanssouci on 17 August 1786.

The schloss is tiny and intimate, with a central hall and just five royal apartments to the east and five guest rooms to the west. Because it is so small, there is a timed entry system, so we had to queue up again and wait to get inside. It was jam-packed and difficult to move around in, but it was worth it. The interior, particularly the Marble Hall and the King's Apartments, is a jewel of flamboyant rococo decoration.

Frederick the Great was very involved in the design of Sanssouci palace and also in the layout of the park that grew up around it. Over the next decades, the park extended along either side of the main avenue, which runs for two kilometres in a straight line to the west and ends at the Neues Palais. Scattered in the park are other historic buildings, including the Picture Gallery, the Orangerie, and the Roman Baths. Our favourite was the gorgeous Chinese House, built in the 1750s in chinoiserie style, where Frederick sometimes took his meals.

25. Frederick (centre) in 1741, at the beginning of his reign.

Neues Palais

We left Sanssouci palace and walked along the long main avenue to visit the Neues Palais (or New Palace). As this, originally small in the distance, got nearer and nearer, we were struck by the difference between the two. While Sanssouci is small, intimate, and charming, the Neues Palais is huge, monumental, and impressive. One of the later buildings in the park, it was built by Frederick the Great in baroque style in the 1760s to host formal state occasions and to show that Prussia was rich and powerful after the Seven Years' War. The main building is over 200 metres long with 200 rooms, and behind it is another enormous building called the Communs, apparently built to hide a swamp. This

26. The Neues Palais was built to show the wealth and power of Prussia.

was the service building for the palace, housing kitchens, laundries, and offices. Today it is part of Potsdam University.

After the death of Frederick the Great, the Neues Palais was hardly used until it became the much-loved summer home of Vicky and Fritz in 1859. In the winter they lived in the Kronprinzenpalais in Berlin and in summer at the Neues Palais in Potsdam. As soon as they moved in, they began to renovate the interiors, using Vicky's annual grant from the British Parliament. She was insistent about installing plumbing, turning the old powder rooms (where occupants retired to powder their wigs) into bathrooms and toilets. When Fritz became emperor, they renamed the palace Friedrichskron in honour of the two Friedrichs who had played such an important role in its history—Friedrich II, who built the palace, and Friedrich III, who restored it.

Vicky and Fritz waited a long time to come to the throne. Their tragedy was that when Fritz did eventually succeed, he was already a man dying from cancer of the larynx. His reign would last only 99 days, and he was too weak from his illness to make any of the changes or push through any of the reforms that he and Vicky had planned. He even had no choice but to confirm the hated Bismarck as his chancellor.

When the news of his father's death came in March 1888, Vicky and Fritz were in Italy, where they had spent the winter in a warmer climate. The new kaiser and kaiserin returned to Germany and to the home they loved the best, the Neues Palais. Fritz died there on the morning of 15 June 1888. When Vicky came out into the garden later to cut roses to put on his body, she found the palace had been cordoned off by soldiers on the orders of her son, the new Kaiser Wilhelm II. Mother and son had a difficult relationship, and he claimed it was necessary to prevent his mother sending state documents to England.

27. The dying Kaiser Friedrich III during his short reign; he died at the Neues Palais.

From the start, the new Kaiser Wilhelm made it clear that he regarded himself as the successor of his grandfather rather than of his father. He told his mother that she would have to leave the Neues Palais, as he needed it himself. Vicky wrote bitterly to her mother:

> Wilhelm II succeeds Wilhelm I...the sooner he (Fritz) is forgotten the better, therefore the sooner his widow disappears the better also.[20]

She thought the alternative homes that he offered her were inadequate and was bitterly upset when her son changed the name back to the Neues Palais from Friedrichskron. Vicky went on to build her own new summer home at Kronberg, which we would visit later in our tour.

Vicky and Fritz are buried in the Kaiser Friedrich III mausoleum in Sanssouci Park, together with their two sons who died as children, Prince Sigismund and Prince Waldemar. We found the mausoleum, but this was not open to the public.

Because of my long-standing interest in Vicky, I had much looked forward to visiting the Neues Palais. However, it was a mixed experience, the main problem for us being the slipperiness of the floors. Visitors are required to wear large and cumbersome felt slippers to protect these, and we slipped and slid around and generally felt insecure on our feet. We wondered how the slippers would pass a health and safety risk assessment! Of course, we understood the need to protect the beautiful floors, but an easy and far safer solution would have been to put down a strip of carpet for visitors to walk on.

In addition, in contrast to most other schlösser that we visited on our tour, the museum attendants at the Neues Palais did not seem very visitor friendly. Our tickets and photo permit were checked multiple times, and we were several times told where not to go. There was a problem when we stopped to look at the wonderful painting of Kaiser Wilhelm I's coronation in Königsberg by Adolf von Menzel. All the royal family and other notables are included in this, and a key is provided for visitors as to who is who. As we leant forward to look at this, an attendant shouted at us. We still don't know what we did wrong. Since the key is displayed under Perspex, it is hard to imagine what damage we could have done.

Charlottenburg

Our next schloss was Charlottenburg, on the outskirts of Berlin. This is where Queen Victoria came in spring 1888 to visit her son-in-law, the dying emperor Friedrich III, of whom she was very fond. In the guidebook to the schloss there is a woodcut by R. Tailor showing her driving up in a carriage[21].

28. Queen Victoria arrives at Charlottenburg.

The schloss was originally built in the 1690s as a small summer home for Sophie Charlotte, then the electress of Brandenburg. Sophie Charlotte was the daughter of Electress Sophia of Hannover and from childhood was always known by the nickname Figuelotte. She married Friedrich III, elector of Brandenburg, as his second wife in 1684. Her first babies did not survive long, but in 1688 she gave birth to an heir, the future King Friedrich Wilhelm I, and she was the grandmother of Frederick the Great. (See family tree 5 for the ancestry of Frederick the Great.) Like her mother, Figuelotte was an intelligent and independent woman, and she held her own court at Charlottenburg, away from the intrigues of Berlin.

Figuelotte's husband was the ruler of two principalities, being both the elector of Brandenburg, which was within the Holy Roman Empire, and the duke of neighbouring Prussia, which was not. When he wanted to upgrade his status and become a king, a deal was done. The emperor could not tolerate a new king within the Holy Roman Empire, as this might threaten his prerogative. But Prussia, being outside the empire, was another matter. In 1701, Elector Friedrich III of Brandenburg became King Friedrich I in Prussia, and thenceforth the Hohenzollerns took this as their senior title. The unusual wording of 'in' Prussia (rather than 'of' Prussia) was significant, to delineate the new king's status. The first king 'of' Prussia was the grandson of Friedrich I, Fredrick the Great.

Friedrich, Figuelotte, and the entire court decamped in an enormous baggage train from Berlin to Königsberg, the capital of Prussia (now Kaliningrad), for the coronation, setting the tradition for future Hohenzollern monarchs to be crowned here. And the schloss at Charlottenburg was enlarged and altered to make it a royal residence worthy of the name. From this period dates the wonderful porcelain cabinet, a room designed to glorify the new kingdom and whose walls are lined by endless pieces of beautiful porcelain. The schloss was originally called Lietzenburg, but when Sophie Charlotte died in 1705, aged 37, her husband renamed it Charlottenburg in her honour.

29. Charlottenburg was named in honour of Sophie Charlotte, the first queen in Prussia.

The palace was popular with the royal family as a summer residence. It was enlarged again by Frederick the Great when he succeeded in 1740, and he lived there until Sanssouci palace was built. It was also later a favourite with King Friedrich Wilhelm III and his wife, Queen Luise.

We arrived at Charlottenburg early in the morning and, benefiting from our experience at Sanssouci, decided not to join the queue for entry to the main palace but to walk first round the gardens. Here we found the mausoleum of Luise, the most famous queen of Prussia.

Princess Luise of Mecklenburg-Strelitz was born in 1776 in Hannover, where her father was regent on behalf of his brother-in-law, George III of Great Britain and Ireland. She was brought up first in Hannover and then, after her mother died and the family was split up, by her maternal grandmother in Hesse-Darmstadt. On Christmas Eve 1793, the 17-year-old Luise was married in Berlin to Crown Prince

Friedrich Wilhelm of Prussia. A few days later, her 15-year-old sister, Friederike, was married to his brother, Prince Luis.

The marriages were arranged by their families. The story goes that when Friedrich Wilhelm met the two sisters, he was uncertain which one to choose as his wife. So, he asked his brother, Luis, which one he wanted, but Luis was indifferent and said he would take whichever sister was left. Friedrich Wilhelm was by nature hesitant, but on the advice of friends, he decided on the elder and more modest Luise rather than her younger sister, Friederike, who he described as more 'seductive'.[22]

Luise and Friederike became Prussia's most famous sisters and were known as the Two Graces. There are many paintings of them including a charming one at Charlottenburg, by Friedrich Weitsch in 1795, in which they are placing a laurel wreath on a bust of their father-in-law, King Friedrich Wilhelm II. And a small porcelain reproduction of the famous life-size marble statue of the pair, of a similar date, by Johann Schadow, is still one of the porcelain factory's best sellers.

30. The Two Graces—Queen Luise and her sister, Friederike, who later became queen of Hannover.

Luise was fortunate in her arranged marriage. She and the crown prince made a good partnership and grew to love each other. There is a tender 1800 portrait of the pair, again by Weitsch, in which they are standing in the garden at Charlottenburg holding hands. Unfaithful husbands were pretty much par for the course in arranged royal marriages, but there has never been any suggestion that Friedrich Wilhelm was unfaithful to Luise. His father's amatory exploits, which involved divorce, a long-standing mistress, and two bigamist morganatic marriages, disgusted his son, who reacted against them. Friedrich Wilhelm had endured a difficult childhood and felt unloved by his parents. He grew up reticent and indecisive, and the more charming and intelligent Luise was his support and backbone. The couple were not often apart, and when they were, Luise still encouraged him and stiffened his resolve. For example, on one occasion when they were separated, she wrote to him:

> I beg you, when you see these gentlemen to arm yourself with courage and steadfastness and tell them gently, but firmly, "This is what I wish".[23]

They became King Friedrich Wilhelm III and Queen Luise in 1797. The couple were popular in Prussia and lived fairly modestly (for royalty), enjoying most the time they spent in their country home in the village of Paretz. Friedrich Wilhelm and Luise had ten children, two of whom were later kings of Prussia (Friedrich Wilhelm IV and his brother, Wilhelm I). All the future kings of Prussia and emperors of Germany were descended from them. (See family tree 6 for the descendants of Friedrich Wilhelm III and Queen Luise.)

Friederike was not as lucky in marriage as her sister. It is thought that her husband, Prince Luis, had been in love with someone else before but was unable to marry his love because she was not of equal birth. He was indifferent to Friederike and unfaithful to her. They had three children, but the marriage was never happy. Luis died from diphtheria in 1796, leaving the 18-year-old Friederike a widow. Her subsequent marital career was somewhat colourful. In 1797 she became unofficially engaged to Prince Adolphus, Duke of Cambridge, a son of King George III and Queen Charlotte, but this had to be broken off when his parents refused their consent. The following year, she became pregnant by Prince Solms-Braunfels and had to lose her title of Royal Highness and leave Berlin and her children to marry him. Sadly, the baby lived only a few months. The couple had three further sons, but the marriage was not a success.

When her third husband, Ernest Duke of Cumberland, another son of George III, met and fell in love with her in 1813, Friederike started divorce proceedings against Prince Solms. He conveniently died in the course of these, making her a widow and saving her the social stigma of divorce. Friederike and Ernest were married in 1815, and in 1819 their son, George (later the blind king of Hannover), was born. However, because of her previous marital history and reputation, her mother-in-law and aunt, Queen Charlotte, always refused to receive her. Ernest and Friederike became king and queen of Hannover in 1837. Friederike's last marriage was the most successful of the three. Ernest told her that his first sight of her

was the most beautiful and happiest moment of my life.[24]

When she died 28 years later, he genuinely mourned her.

Tragedy came to Prussia when Napoleon invaded in October 1806. Friedrich Wilhelm had dithered too long and mishandled the crisis. His Austrian allies had already been defeated, and his Russian allies were unable to assist him. The much vaunted Prussian army built up by Frederick the Great and his father, turned out to be a thing of the past and no match for Napoleon's more modern methods of warfare. Thousands of Prussians died on the battlefields of Jena-Auerstadt. Luise followed the Prussian army to war in a carriage until she was turned back on the eve of battle. She fled first to Berlin and then with her family, as Napoleon advanced to occupy the capital, into East Prussia and to Königsberg, the ancient capital on the Baltic Sea.

The following year, after the defeat of Russia, Emperor Alexander and Napoleon met for a peace conference at Tilsit (now Sovetsk). The conference is remembered partly because their meeting was stage-managed and took place on a raft moored in the centre of the Niemen River. Friedrich Wilhelm, who was also at the conference, was faced with very harsh terms for Prussia. He asked his wife to come to Tilsit in the hope that she could persuade Napoleon to be more generous. Luise dressed in all her finery for Napoleon. She met with him alone, but although he was courteous, her intervention was not successful. Only a fraction of Prussia was given back to Friedrich Wilhelm, and this was still occupied by the French, pending payment of a large indemnity. Luise sold her jewellery and melted down her gold plate to help pay this off. Only in December 1809 did the royal family return to Berlin.

During the years of the Napoleonic Wars, Luise was often ill and suffered from a heart complaint. She died aged 34, worn out by war and childbirth, in July 1810. Her bereaved and grieving husband had a mausoleum built to remember her at Charlottenburg, in one of her favourite parts of the garden at the end of a long avenue of firs. She was interred there a few months after her death.

31. The mausoleum of Queen Luise in the schoss garden at Charlottenburg.

How Germany Was United Under Prussia

It has been calculated that at the time of the Peace of Westphalia in 1648, which brought to an end the devastating conflict of the Thirty Years' War, the Holy Roman Empire was splintered into nearly 1800 different pieces of territory[25]. These comprised not only principalities ruled by a duke or count but also ecclesiastical territories ruled by a prince-bishop or abbot, and free towns and cities that had self-governing rights. Many of these territories were very small in size.

Over the next centuries the number of territories reduced, and there was a major shake-up in the early 1800s as a result of Napoleon and the French wars. Starting in 1803, the process of secularisation and mediatisation was originally designed to compensate German rulers for the loss of their lands to the west of the Rhine that had been annexed by France but became much more wide-reaching. Under the process of secularisation virtually all the ecclesiastical lands were parcelled out among the secular princes; only a very few, such as the archbishopric of Mainz, remained. The free cities also lost their independent status and were amalgamated into neighbouring territories; only a handful, such as Hamburg and Frankfurt, kept their status. And under mediatisation rulers of the smaller secular states were forced to cede their principalities to the larger, whilst retaining their schlösser, their titles, and (most importantly) their equal marriage status. At the end of the process, the 1800 pieces of the old Holy Roman Empire had been reduced to less than 50.

The Congress of Vienna in 1815, at the end of the Napoleonic Wars, further rationalised the number of independent states in the new German Federation to 39, (comprising 35 independent states and four free cities). The impact of Napoleon on the structure of Germany was therefore enormous. Generally speaking it was the larger states who were the winners, seeing an increase in their territory and an elevation in their title; for example, the elector of Hannover became a king and the landgrave of Hesse-Darmstadt a grand duke.

Another legacy of the struggle against Napoleon was a growing movement within Germany for a united country under the leadership of Prussia. This *was ultimately achieved as a result of war under the 'blood and iron' policies of Bismarck rather than by diplomacy. Its defeat by Prussia in the Seven Weeks' War of 1866 finally forced Austria out of German affairs and other German states that had sided with Austria, such as Hannover and Nassau, were annexed by Prussia and lost their sovereignty. The victory over France in the Franco-Prussian War of 1870 generated the national enthusiasm and pride that led to the king of Prussia being acclaimed as kaiser (or emperor) of a united Germany by the other ruling German princes in a ceremony that took place in the Hall of Mirrors at Versailles Palace near Paris in 1871.*

The fame of Queen Luise has endured to this day, partly because of her youth and beauty, but also because of the role she played at Tilsit. Her meeting with Napoleon achieved little, but the legend of the queen courageously appealing to the enemy on behalf of her country has caught the public imagination.

We were the first visitors of the day to this mausoleum in the schloss garden at Charlottenburg. In the style of a Doric temple, it is a lovely and peaceful place. It is possible to go inside, and a more-than-helpful museum attendant showed us how to buy a ticket from the ticket machine. Four white marble grave statues fill the hall of remembrance; they are of Luise, her husband, their son, Kaiser Wilhelm I, and his wife, Augusta of Saxe-Weimar-Eisenach. In life, Wilhelm I revered his mother and was a regular visitor to her mausoleum. He visited the night before he left for another war with France in 1870, which ended with the defeat of Napoleon's nephew, Napoleon III, and resulted in Wilhelm becoming the first kaiser of a united Germany.

Friedrich Wilhelm III did not marry again until 1824, when he made a morganatic marriage to Auguste von Harrach, Princess Leignitz, and built the New Pavilion in the garden at Charlottenburg as their private retreat. This was one of our favourite places on our tour. The pavilion is small and quiet and felt very private, and the attendants were helpful and friendly and showed interest in our questions. We formed the view that the fewer visitors, the more welcoming the staff. The museum contents were very well displayed, with some helpful English translation. There are family portraits and busts and an interesting exhibition of the history of the building and interiors. There is also, to my husband's great delight, a whole room full of paintings by his favourite artist, the German romantic landscape painter, Caspar David Friedrich (1744-1840). At home we have a copy of his charming small painting of *Swans in the Reeds* painted for us by a graduate of the St. Petersburg Academy of Arts, with the permission of the State Hermitage Museum, where the original hangs.

On the night of 22 November 1943 large parts of Charlottenburg, including the New Pavilion, were destroyed or damaged in a bombing raid. Fortunately much of the contents had already been moved elsewhere for safekeeping. Restoration work began in phases in the 1950s and was completed in the 1990s.

Paretz

32. Schloss Paretz, the favourite home of Friedrich Wilhelm III and Queen Luise.

Our favourite in the Berlin and Brandenburg area was Schloss Paretz, the country home of Friedrich Wilhelm III and Luise. The king chose this place because he had been happy here as a child, living with the family of Count von Blumenthal, who was governor to his brother. In 1795, he bought the estate from the count's son and turned it into a royal retreat. The schloss is a long, low, modest building that the royal couple furnished with contemporary furniture and special painted and printed wallpaper. They also redesigned the whole village as a sort of model farming community.

The royal family came here for a few weeks every summer and tried to live the life of an ordinary country family. The king particularly liked to be here for the high point of the village year, which was Harvest Festival, when he led the festivities

33. Friedrich Wilhelm III survived his first wife by thirty years – the mausoleum of Queen Luise is shown in the background of his portrait.

and entertained his neighbours. The young Helena Paulowna, duchess of Mecklenburg-Schwerin, was a happy guest here for Harvest Festival a year before her early death in 1803. Paretz village is still much as it must have been then—a quiet country place. We were there on a sunny day in May, and we sat outside the village inn eating our lunch. The asparagus was in season, and like every eating place in Germany, there was a special *spargel* (white asparagus) menu. I ate masses of it on our tour, with hollandaise sauce, of course.

Paretz was little used after Queen Luise died, but it remained in the ownership of the Hohenzollern family until 1918. It was hard to determine the building's history over the ensuing decades, as there was little information available in English. It was apparently occupied by the Red Army, used to house refugees, and served as an agricultural college. At some point, the interior was altered and the famous wallpaper removed. It opened as a museum in 2001, and an exhibition charts the progress of the restoration from 1999. The wallpaper is back in place and is quite delightful.

Cecilienhof

34. Cecilienhof is modelled on an English country house.

Our final visit in the area was to Cecilienhof, built during World War I as a summer home for Crown Prince Wilhelm and his wife, Cecilie of Mecklenburg-Schwerin. This is in a lovely spot on the side of Lake Jungfernsee in Potsdam. It is enormous and rambling, built round three internal courtyards in mock Tudor style.

The Iron Curtain and Germany

The Iron Curtain is a name for the ideological and political barrier that divided Europe into East and West after World War II. The term was used colourfully by British Prime Minister Winston Churchill in postwar rhetoric warning of the threat of communism.

> *From Stettin in the Baltic to Trieste in the Adriatic an Iron Curtain has descended across the continent.*[26]

After Germany's defeat in 1945, the victorious Allies divided Germany into four occupied zones—American, British, French, and Soviet. The city of Berlin, over 100 miles inside the Soviet zone, was also similarly divided. This division into East and West eventually became permanent with the setting up in 1949 of two separate countries, the Federal Republic of Germany (West Germany) with its capital in Bonn, and the German Democratic Republic or GDR (East Germany) with its capital in East Berlin.

The Iron Curtain between the countries was also a physical barrier. I can remember driving out to see the border in the countryside on a visit to West Germany in 1981. The sight was startling, like something from a film, with high fences, watch towers, border guards, and a 'no go' zone. It was threatening and quite frightening, and I was glad to drive away.

Cecilienhof was built to the highest standards and with all the latest comforts of the day. The couple wanted it to have the feel of an English country house. At the time of our visit it was a hotel and restaurant, as well as a museum, and surrounded by well-kept, pretty, English-style gardens.

The crown prince was away with his battalion on the Western Front, but Crown Princess Cecilie moved into the new schloss in August 1917, just in time for the birth of her sixth and final child, Princess Cecilia. After the fall of the Prussian monarchy in 1918, the property of the Hohenzollern family was confiscated by the new Prussian state. The crown prince was exiled to the Dutch island of Wieringen, but the crown princess decided to stay in Germany with her children. The ownership of Cecilienhof was disputed until, under the 'princes' settlement' of 1926, it was decided that the schloss was owned by the state but that the family could live there.

35. Crown Prince Wilhelm and Crown Princess Cecilie at the start of World War I.

In her memoirs, Cecilie said that their five years of separation, when her husband was in exile, were hard on them both. This may have been a gloss on the truth, as the marriage was almost certainly not happy. The cracks had begun early on, fuelled by the serial infidelity of the crown prince. Cecilie was the only senior ex-royal to stay in Germany, and during these years she assumed responsibilities and became matriarch of the family, a position that she refused to give up after her husband's return[27].

Her memoirs are remarkably jolly and positive for a woman who had her share of misfortune, including, as well as an unhappy marriage and the loss of a throne, a daughter born with Down's syndrome (although this was never acknowledged publically), and later on a son killed in battle in World War II. Only a few pages are chilling, where in accordance with views held in Germany at the time, she totally rejected any German responsibility for causing the horrors of World War I and attempted to whitewash the image of her father-in-law, the kaiser. She said that anyone who knew him

> would be unable to understand to his dying day how war propaganda could have succeeded in presenting my father-in-law to the world as responsible for the war! Never has a greater and more shameful lie been spread through the world, and never has the honour of a great and peace-loving nation been more wantonly defamed than in this accusation, which was then actually upheld in a so-called "Treaty!".[28]

The family continued to occupy Cecilienhof until forced to leave quickly in spring 1945. Much was left behind, which is one reason why the schloss is so interesting to visit today. I particularly liked the sitting room of the crown princess, modelled after a ship's cabin. Apparently she was interested in navigation and loved to go cruising!

Cecilienhof is most famous as the location for the Potsdam conference in July 1945, when the Big Three met for peace talks and to decide the future of Europe. The Great Hall was turned into a conference room. Stalin used the crown princess's study, Truman the crown prince's smoking room, and Churchill, later Atlee, the library. After the division of Germany, Cecilienhof was located in the GDR but was very close to the border with West Berlin. Between 1961 and 1989, the Berlin Wall ran through the gardens. Within sight of the schloss were all the border paraphernalia, including a six-metre-high fence, the concrete wall, a death strip, watchtowers, a dog run, and a road for the border troops.

There is an extensive exhibition in the museum about the war, the peace conference, and the dropping of the atom bombs, all translated into English. There were many visitors to this, mostly Germans but also several coach parties of Japanese.

Cecilienhof was a pleasure to visit, but it does seem something of an oddity. The schloss was built during World War I, when Germany was engaged in a terrible war with England, yet it was modelled on an English country house and garden.

Cecilie's father-in-law, Wilhelm II, was the last kaiser. He was the son of an English mother and the grandson of Queen Victoria, and he always had a love-hate relationship with his mother's country. Perhaps Cecilienhof, the last schloss built before the German monarchy was abolished in 1918, reflects this split personality.

36. World War I was raging when Cecilienhof was built – original sketch of Kaiser Wilhelm II.

The Berlin Wall

The most potent symbol of the Iron Curtain and the Cold War was the Berlin Wall, which was erected by the East German government in 1961 to seal off West Berlin and prevent the steady flow of its citizens to the West. The wall ran through some of the most historic parts of the city, notably the Brandenburg Gate, and almost overnight it separated families and friends. It has been estimated that in the 28 years of its existence over 100 East Germans died as they desperately tried to cross the wall to reach the West. The first deaths were within days of the wall going up, the last in February 1989.

The Berlin Wall vanished as quickly as it had been put up. On 9 November 1989 the crumbling East German regime announced freedom of travel for its citizens to the West. It was a hugely emotional night in Berlin, as the crossing points were opened, and East Berliners streamed across to be greeted by cheering Westerners. The events were broadcast live, and driving home in London I stopped my car to listen on the radio; it was a world-changing moment.

Today it is hard to spot the exact route of the wall in Berlin; only a few memorials, such as Checkpoint Charlie, remain. The border between East and West Germany is still marked, however. Driving along the major roads we saw several signs marking the 'Inner Deutscher Grenze', or intra-German border, as we crossed the old border between West and East.

5

SAXONY AND THE WETTINS

For our next stop on our schloss tour we drove further south to the state of Saxony (Sachsen) and its capital city, Dresden. The weather continued to be wonderful. When we left home in England, it was cold, grey, and rainy. In Germany it was dry and sunny, with temperatures rising in Dresden to more than 25 degrees centigrade. It rained only once, when we were in a restaurant having dinner!

Saxony is a landlocked state in northeast Germany, surrounded by other German states which were also part of the GDR, and bordering Poland and the Czech Republic to the east. Located at the centre of Europe it has a rich royal history, and for 500 years was ruled by the Wettin dynasty. Like other ancient noble families, the Wettin were prone to divide and reorganise their lands, but the most important of their possesions was the kingdom of Saxony, which they held from the 15th century until the end of the German monarchy. (For a brief summary of the Wettins, please see appendix A on the royal families and main historical characters.)

Residenzschloss

37. The Residenzschloss in Dresden houses the famous Green Vaults.

In Saxony our hotel was in the centre of Dresden, near the Residenzschloss, or royal palace. Dresden is a beautiful baroque city built by Saxon Elector Friedrich August I and his son, Friedrich August II, who together transformed it into a centre of art and culture. Close together in the centre are many famous sites, including the August Bridge, the Semper Opera House, the Zwinger, and the Frauenkirche (Church of Our Lady). As we walked around this lovely area, it was sobering to think that it was all destroyed towards the end of World War II. On the night of 13 February 1945, there was an Anglo-American bombing raid on Dresden and 25,000 people were killed in the raid and the firestorm that followed it.

Queen Elizabeth II of Great Britain toured this area of Dresden during her historic first visit to the old GDR in October 1992. The visit was initially tense, as no one was sure how the people of Dresden would react. As her car drove past the ruins of the Frauenkirche, the crowds were silent, and some eggs were thrown. During the visit, however, the mood changed to one of reconciliation, and later there were large, cheering crowds to greet her when she arrived by train in Leipzig[29]. Today the centre of Dresden has risen again like a phoenix from the ashes. The historic buildings have been rebuilt, and the streets are buzzing and full of tourists.

The Residenzschloss was built in stages from the 15th to the 17th centuries and was the seat of government of the Wettin family, who were first dukes, then electors, and then kings of Saxony. After the war, restoration work began in the 1960s and is now largely complete. Today the schloss houses the famous Grunes Gewolbe (Green Vaults), a vast collection of royal jewels and treasures. It also has the best museum bookshop of any that we found on our tour.

In the former royal stables is the Long Walk, which houses an amazing porcelain artwork. This is the 102-metre-long mural of a

38. Portrait of Augustus the Strong in the Furstenzug (Procession of Princes).

mounted procession of the rulers of Saxony called the Furstenzug, or Procession of Princes. It was originally painted in the 1870s but was transferred to 25,000 Meissen porcelain tiles in the early 1900s to make it more durable. It is the largest porcelain artwork in the world.

This wonderful mural shows 35 dukes, electors, and kings of Saxony from the 12th century until 1904. The last king shown is Georg, who reigned from 1902 to 1904. He was succeeded by his son, Friedrich August III, the last king of Saxony, who is shown in his father's retinue. We thoroughly enjoyed walking along the length of the procession and took masses of photographs.

Taschenbergpalais

We stayed in the Taschenbergpalais, which is next to the Residenzschloss and is now a hotel. It was built in the early 1700s by Elector Friedrich August I of Saxony for his mistress, Countess Cosel. He had a private covered bridge built to connect his palace and the Taschenberg, so he could visit his mistress in private without having to cross the street.

Elector Friedrich August I is better known to history as August der Starke, or Augustus the Strong. He is without doubt the most famous monarch of Saxony, and we saw his name and image everywhere in Dresden. Born as the younger son of Elector Johann Georg III in 1670, he succeeded to the Saxon throne unexpectedly in 1694, when his elder brother (Elector Johann Georg IV) died of smallpox. Augustus was elector of Saxony for 39 years until his death and was also elected king of Poland, as August II, in 1697. He earned his nickname both because of his physical strength (he could apparently roll up a heavy silver plate as if it were a piece of paper), but also because under his reign, Saxony became one of the strongest German states. An absolute ruler who spent millions pursuing an opulent lifestyle and his Polish dream, Augustus also built up the Saxon army and was a reformer. He introduced a form of cabinet government in Saxony and made

39. The Taschenbergpalais was built by Augustus the Strong for his mistress, Countess Cosel.

economic and fiscal reforms, including the first-ever consumption tax (now known as VAT), which made him independent of the aristocracy.

Augustus was a notorious womaniser; he had a series of mistresses and was rumoured to have hundreds of illegitimate children, although this was certainly an exaggeration. One that he acknowledged was the famous Maurice de Saxe who, without an inheritance, forged a glittering career as a soldier of fortune and ended up as a Maréchal of France. Maurice's mother was Aurora von Königsmarck, a Swedish beauty and the sister of Count Philippe von Königsmarck. She led the fruitless search for her brother when he disappeared one night in 1694 on his way to see his clandestine lover, Sophie Dorothee of Celle (see Schloss Ahlden).

Augustus's most famous mistress was Anna Constantia, Countess Cosel. Anna Constantia was still married to the head of the tax collection service for Saxony, Adolf von Hoym, when she met Augustus and became his mistress in 1704 or 1705. Her rise in the world was then rapid; she was made a countess in 1706 and moved into her own palace, the Taschenberg, in 1707. That same year, Augustus also gave her a summer palace outside Dresden on the banks of the Elbe. The couple had three children together, daughters born in 1708 and 1709 and a son born in 1712. (See family tree 7 for information on Augustus the Strong and Countess Cosel.)

Anna Constantia was very beautiful and also clever and ambitious. Before becoming Augustus's mistress, she managed to extract a promise of marriage from him, which was put down in a written document. It seems that she was not content to be the king's mistress but wanted to take the place of his wife. She also expressed her own political views, which did not always agree with those of Augustus. Like many of his subjects, she was against his being king of Poland because of the cost to Saxon revenues and because it was a Catholic country. Saxony was Protestant, but in an opportunistic move, Augustus had converted to Catholicism in order to be eligible for election to the Polish throne. On the other side to the Taschenbergpalais, the Residenzschloss is connected to the Catholic Hofkirche.

After several years as the king's mistress, Countess Cosel suddenly fell from favour. She then made some serious mistakes that would have an adverse impact on her future. She refused to go out of the king's life quietly. She tried to use the written document from the start of their relationship to blackmail Augustus, and she fled to the Prussian court to do this. She ought to have realised that monarchs are more powerful than ex-mistresses and that in these types of matters, they tend to stick together. Prussia returned Anna Constantia to Saxony, the fortune that she had accumulated as Augustus's mistress was confiscated, and she was sent to prison at Stolpen.

The Taschenbergpalais reverted to the king and was refurbished for Augustus's son (also Friedrich August) and new daughter-in-law, Archduchess Maria Josepha of Austria. It remained a residence for the Saxon royal family until 1918, when the last king abdicated.

JAN. 3. 1903   *BLACK AND WHITE BUDGET*   453

* THE RUNAWAY ROYALTIES *

Princess Louise of Saxony has run away with a French tutor from her husband, the Crown Prince, while her brother, the Archduke Leopold Frederick, accompanies her in exile with his own friend, an actress

40. When Luise of Saxony ran away from her husband it caused a sensational scandal that was covered in the international press.

It was from the Taschenberg that Crown Princess Luise left when she ran away from Saxony and her husband in December 1902. She went openly to her parents' home in Salzburg and then secretly on to Switzerland, where she met up with her children's tutor, and the story of her flight broke in the press. She became an overnight sensation, with her continuing story being reported in detail and followed by readers everywhere.

Luise was born an archduchess of Hapsburg-Tuscany, the daughter of Grand Duke Ferdinand IV of Tuscany. She married Prince Friedrich August of Saxony in 1891. The couple became crown prince and princess in June 1902. Luise was popular in Saxony and got on reasonably well with her husband, but she was unconventional for a princess, became frustrated by the etiquette of the Saxon court, and did not fit in with her in-laws. She ran away because she feared imprisonment when her father-in-law, King Georg, claimed she was unbalanced and threatened to have her committed to a lunatic asylum. Luise did not regard it as an empty threat. She may have had in mind the example of Princess Louise, the daughter of King Leopold II of Belgium, who was institutionalised by her father in 1898 after she left her husband for her lover. Louise was shut up for six years, until she escaped from the asylum in 1904, with the help of her lover[30].

In 1911, Luise published her autobiography. She wrote:

> I knew that my hours of personal liberty were numbered at Dresden, and that any appeal to my husband would be worse than useless. There was nothing for me but flight.[31]

Luise left her six children behind and was pregnant with a seventh when she ran away. She had hoped to continue to see them, but the king did not allow this. When her father-in-law died in 1904, Luise returned secretly to Dresden to try to see her children. She was arrested at the door of the Taschenberg, however, before she could do so. And several years later, she had to give over her last child, her daughter, Monica, born after she ran away, to be brought up at the Saxon court.

Luise was divorced from the crown prince in 1903 by royal decree of her father-in-law. Her relationship with the tutor was short-lived, but in 1907 she married the musician, Enrico Toselli. The couple had a son, but again the relationship did not last, and they divorced in 1912. (See family tree 8 for the marriages of Luise, Crown Princess of Saxony.) Her first husband, who became King Friedrich August III on the death of his father, never remarried. The Saxon royal family had remained Catholic since the conversion of Augustus the Strong. Friedrich still regarded Luise as his wife and may have had a lingering affection for her. He was the last king of Saxony.

After 1918, the Taschenberg Palace was used for a variety of purposes, including a physiotherapy clinic and a tinned food factory. It was destroyed in the 1945 bombing raid, and only a part of the front façade was left standing. After the war there were calls to knock this down, too, but in the event it was propped up and made safe to wait until reconstruction could begin. Reconstruction began in 1993, and after just a swift two years, the Taschenbergpalais Hotel opened in 1995.

In August 2002, the centre of Dresden suffered another disaster when the Elbe overflowed its banks in what became known as the flood of the century. The hotel was flooded out, thousands of tons of filthy water inundated the cellars and lower floors, and the guests had to be evacuated. There was extensive damage, and certain parts of the hotel had to be demolished and rebuilt. Even the wine in the cellars was lost when all the labels floated off. Not knowing what wine was in each bottle, the owners had to give it away. The hotel reopened for business after just a few weeks, but the threat still remains. Just a month after we were there, in June 2013, the city was again on high flood alert when water levels in the Elbe rose five metres higher than normal. Thankfully, this time the water levels fell, and the threatened flood did not materialise.

41. The schloss church next to the Taschenbergpalais in Dresden.

What Was Morganatic Marriage?

The concept of morganatic marriage was developed to recognise marriages between partners of unequal social status. In most cases the husband was of royal birth and his wife of a lower social standing, although occasionally it was the other way around. The marriage did not confer royal rank or precedence on the wife or children of the marriage, and they had limited rights of inheritance. It was sometimes called a 'left-handed marriage' because the bridegroom gave the bride his left hand in the wedding ceremony rather than the right.

One of the most famous morganatic marriages was that between Archduke Franz Ferdinand, heir to the Austrian empire, and Countess Sophie Chotek, who were assassinated together in Sarajevo in June 1914 triggering the series of events that led to World War I. Sophie was from a wealthy and aristocratic family but was not of royal rank. The couple had to surmount huge barriers before they were eventually allowed to marry, and a recent book marking the centenary of their deaths tells of the many petty humiliations inflicted on Sophie by the hidebound Austrian court[32].

The issue of morganatic marriage was often sensitive and sometimes considered to bring disgrace on the family. Prince Francis of Teck always felt that his parents' morganatic marriage had blighted his life since, had his mother been of equal birth, he would have become king of Württemberg. However, this did not prevent his daughter marrying Queen Victoria's grandson to become Queen Mary of Great Britain. In Britain the issue was less sensitive and Queen Victoria held tolerant views. Her youngest daughter married Prince Henry of Battenberg, the son of a morganatic marriage between Prince Alexander of Hesse-Darmstadt and Countess Julie Hauke. One of her granddaughters married his brother, Louis. However when another granddaughter, a princess of Prussia, fell in love with yet a third brother, Alexander, Kaiser Wilhelm II absolutely refused to allow them to marry.

The issue continues to trouble some of the ex-ruling houses even today. For example, the debate on the leadership of the house of Romanov (until 1917 Tsars of Russia) involves consideration of whether certain marriages were or were not morganatic and whether the children had dynastic rights.

Burg Stolpen

42. Stolpen was a remote Wettin castle when Countess Cosel
was imprisoned there.

We returned to the story of Countess Cosel when we visited Burg
Stolpen, around 30 kilometres east of Dresden. This is where she was
imprisoned after her return from Prussia. At the time, Stolpen was a
remote Wettin castle that had not been used for many years other than
on the occasional hunting trip. Here she was guarded by soldiers and
was not allowed to leave or receive visitors or even write letters. She
saw no one except her few servants. It was a very different life than she
had been used to as Augustus's favourite. The burg is a fortress rather
than a grand palace, and she lived in rather Spartan accommodation in
a narrow, fortified tower. Anna Constantia was imprisoned there for 49
years, until her death in 1765.

Countess Cosel's story has inspired writers in the centuries since
her death. One of the first to write about her was the celebrated
polish writer, Joseph J. Kraszewski. In his 1873 novel, he portrayed
the imprisoned countess as a bitter and disillusioned, but still proud,
woman. Despite heavy pressure, she refuses to give up the king's

written promise of marriage as, without this, she would be just another of his many discarded mistresses. She compares herself to these other women:

> No, I am different. I thought there were hearts, souls, consciences; that love was not lechery, that promises ought to be kept, that the King's words were holy. All that was only my illusion. Consequently, while the other women are happy, I am dying of humiliation, longing and shame.[33]

It was a heavy price to pay for her intransigence and foolish actions. Perhaps, in the early years at Stolpen, she hoped that Augustus might forgive her or later when he died in 1733 that she might be released or that her children might come to her rescue. None of these things happened. Kraszewski includes a scene in his novel where Augustus comes to Stolpen in order to test his cannon against the basalt foundations of the schloss. The countess believes that he has come to

43. Countess Cosel, who tried to blackmail her royal lover after their affair ended.

release her and fulfil his promise. When she finds out the truth she is devastated and attempts to kill the king[34].

Anna Constantia died at Stolpen, aged 84, and is buried in the chapel. This is now a ruin, but her grave is still marked by a plaque. Some rooms at the burg are laid out as they might have been while Countess Cosel was there, and there is an exhibition about her life and story.

44. Burg Stolpen is built on a dramatic natural feature—an outcrop of basalt.

Stolpen has another curiosity, which is that the schloss is built on a dramatic natural feature—an outcrop of basalt. This is a volcanic rock, and the columns of basalt that rise vertically from the ground here, rather like hexagonal baulks of timber, were formed about 25 million years ago. The rock was discovered here in 1546 by the founder of the science of mining and mineralogy, Georgius Agricola. He named it

Stolpener basalt, 'basalt' from the Latin for 'very hard', and 'Stolpener' because he found the rock at Stolpen.

The schloss has the deepest basalt well in the world, which is 84 metres deep, and it's still there today. Because the rock is so hard, this took 24 years to dig. The diggers had to light fires on the rock in order to soften it, and progress was extremely slow, at just one to one and a half centimetres a day, or three to four metres a year. When they started digging, no one knew whether they would ever hit water. When the well was completed in 1632, it secured an independent water supply, which was very important to the castle's defence in case of a siege.

We much enjoyed our visit to Stolpen. The construction and layout of the burg are extremely interesting and so is the exhibition about Countess Cosel. There was plenty of information available in English at the ticket office and shop, and a charming and helpful museum attendant. She apologised for her English (although she didn't need to do so, as it was very good) and said that in the GDR years, she had no opportunity to practice it. As it was a hot, sunny day, we relaxed and sat on the terrace outside the café in the inner bailey, drinking coffee.

Pillnitz

We also went to another schloss associated with Countess Cosel. When we had visited Dresden some six years before, in 2007, we arrived at Schloss Pillnitz by water on the paddle steamer from the Bruhl Terrace in Dresden. This is undoubtedly the best way to arrive, as the schloss is located on the bank of, and designed in conjunction with, the Elbe. But this time we drove to it. The schloss is not well signposted, and the car park is small. Surprisingly, we found this to be generally the case everywhere we went, even for those schlösser that are well visited. However, a smiling parking attendant found a vacant corner and fitted us in.

Pillnitz was already a Wettin palace when Augustus gave it to his mistress, Anna Constantia Cosel, as her summer residence in 1707.

45. Pillnitz Palace seen from the Elbe River.

Although only a few kilometres upstream, the palace was remote from Dresden in those days, so that when their affair ended, Augustus first confined her at Pillnitz. It was only after her flight to Berlin and extradition back to Dresden that she was imprisoned more closely at Stolpen. Augustus then repossessed Pillnitz, and in the 1720s, he embarked on a major rebuilding project to create the structure we see today. Augustus used the schloss as a pleasure palace, for occasional court entertainments in summer, when courtiers would play games or ride on carousels and swings. Later, however, it became an official summer residence and a favourite with the Wettin family. Several later kings of Saxony were born, or died, at Pillnitz.

The glory of Pillnitz is the setting and the beautiful gardens. Twin buildings, in Chinese baroque style, face each other across a formal pleasure garden and are surrounded by a large park. The Wasserpalais (Water Palace) is on the bank of the Elbe, with elegant curving steps down to the river. Here Augustus would arrive by water from Dresden in his gondola. A gondola is still on show in the schloss garden. Across the formal garden is the matching Bergpalais, or Upper Palace, with avenues of old lime and chestnut trees behind. Linking the two is a third palace. In Augustus's day this was the original renaissance schloss; today it is the Neuen Palais, which was built about a century later.

Augustus's great-grandson, King Friedrich August I, and great-great-grandson, King Friedrich August II, were both keen botanists and plant collectors. They extended the gardens at Pillnitz and built up a famous plant collection. Although many of the plants were later given to the botanical gardens in Dresden, it is still a beautiful garden and has a large collection of plants in pots, which are brought outdoors in the summer. We saw the gardens at their best, in full spring glory, with the plants in pots on show and the sun shining. Everywhere in Saxony, the lilac was in flower, in a spectrum of colour from white through pale mauve to deep purple. At Pillnitz, there was a lilac garden, with a display of standard lilac trees with twisted trunks in a courtyard behind the Neuen Palais. The lilac was in full bloom, beautiful and scented.

46. Pillnitz has a famous collection of plants in pots.

Pillnitz remained a royal summer residence until the abdication of the last king in 1918, when it passed into state ownership. Between the wars, some rooms were opened to the public, and it also became an artists' colony. During World War II, it fortunately escaped destruction and was used to store art treasures

47. The Bergpalais at Pillnitz.

evacuated from Dresden, many of which were confiscated and sent to the Soviet Union after the war. They were some of many; a list produced by the Soviet Union in 1958 showed a staggering nearly two million works of art that were 'rescued' from Germany and were 'in the Soviet Union for temporary storage'.[35]

In the 1960s, an arts-and-crafts museum opened in the schloss and is still there, housed in the Wasserpalais and the Bergpalais. In 2006, an exhibition of the history of the palace and the Saxon royal family opened in the Neuen Palais.

We visited this exhibition and found it extremely interesting and comprehensive, covering all the electors and kings from Augustus the Strong up to the last king, Friedrich August III. Everything was translated into English, which was very helpful in untangling who succeeded whom and when. I found this confusing for Saxony, as there was not always a linear descent from father to son, with brother often succeeding brother or nephew to uncle. An unusual and very effective feature of the exhibition was a circular, internal, windowless room with a series of lithograph or copperplate portraits of all the monarchs, in date order. We were not sure why these in particular had to be protected from the light, as there seemed to be more fragile or valuable things on show, but we shut ourselves away in the room and enjoyed looking at the portraits.

Colditz

48. An old postcard shows a view of Colditz castle from the River Mulde.

And finally in Saxony, we headed up the Mulde Valley, known as the Valley of the Castles, to visit two impressive schlösser, each of which had a dark time in its history. The first of these was Colditz. This is such a famous place in the UK that it was a must for us to visit. As part of the postwar baby boom generation, my husband and I were brought up on the legend of the famous escapes from the prisoner-of-war camp at Colditz. These were recorded in the 1952 best-selling book, *The Colditz Story*, by Pat Reid, who was the British escape officer in the camp; in the 1955 film of the same name based on this starring John Mills and Eric Portman; and in the TV series of the 1970s, *Colditz*, with David McCallum and Robert Wagner.

Colditz was another schloss that was hard to find. We could not see any signs showing where to park and, after driving round and round, had to stop in the village square and ask directions in a café. Nor was the route from the car park to the schloss well signposted, so we just headed uphill and hoped that it was right.

The museum attendant in the ticket office told us that the schloss still gets many British visitors who want to see where these events took place, and there was plenty of material in English available about this period in the history of the schloss. As we already knew Pat Reid's book quite well, we bought *Colditz: The German Story* by Reinhold Eggers, who was a security officer at the castle for five years and wrote from the point of view of the German guards. My husband read this book during our holiday and was frequently in hoots of laughter over the contents. The prisoners were so ingenious that very often the guards did not know how an escape had been made or indeed whether there had been an escape at all. The prisoners frequently faked the daily headcount or made diversions to distract the guards. Two of them managed to hide secretly in the castle for nearly a year and appeared only for the headcounts to stand in for escapers and delay discovery of their escape. Prisoners also managed to make two quite realistic dummies, named Max and Moritz, which they used on parade to make up the numbers.

The existence of Schloss Colditz is first documented in the 11th century. In its early days, it belonged to the Holy Roman emperor, but it later passed to the Wettin family. Up to the middle of the 18th century, they used it regularly, but then it fell into disuse and disrepair. In 1800, it became a corrective institution, first a workhouse for the destitute, then a mental asylum, and in the 1930s a prison for Jews, homosexuals, and political opponents of the Nazi regime.

From 1939 to 1945, the schloss was a prisoner-of-war camp for British, French, Dutch, Polish, and other officers, known as OFLAG IV C. Colditz was a Sonderlager, or special camp; it was a camp exclusively for officers—only those who had escaped from other camps and were therefore graded high risk were sent to Colditz. Also incarcerated here were the *prominente*—prominent people who were potential hostages. These included Viscount George Lascelles, who was the nephew of George VI, the son of his sister, Mary, the Princess Royal.

The German command considered Colditz to be escape proof, but this proved to be far from true, and the prisoners soon showed that a castle designed and built to keep the enemy out may not be so good at keeping prisoners in. There were attempted escapes on almost a weekly basis. During the years that Colditz was a camp, there were 186 escape attempts, of which 31 were 'home runs', meaning that the escaper made it all the way back home.

49. Colditz evokes strong memories of its days as a famous prisoner-of-war camp.

Walking up the hill from the town and across the bridge to enter the schloss evoked strong memories of its prisoner-of-war camp days as shown in the film and TV series. We walked first through the outer courtyard in the German part of the castle, where the old kommandant's office is now a youth hostel, and then into the inner or prisoners' courtyard, now part of the museum. The museum contents are extremely interesting, and as you might expect, everything is translated into English. The German guards compiled their own escape museum and carefully recorded and photographed all escape attempts that became known to them. They used this to train new staff and also circulated the material to other camps with a warning as to what to look out for. They regarded Colditz as a sort of 'best in class' camp for escapes. Many of these photos are now on show; we saw photographs of ropes made of bed sheets dangling down the wall; entrances and exits to tunnels; and prisoners disguised as women, German guards, and the civilian camp electrician.

Other exhibits show the prisoners' ingenuity and the things they were able to manufacture from odd bits and pieces, things they pilfered or smuggled in, such as a sewing machine made of wood. Even 50 years after the war, there were still further discoveries at the castle. In 1993, workmen found a secret radio room in the attic, built by the prisoners, that had until then been untouched and undiscovered. We liked the watercolours on show painted by the British officer, William Faithfull Anderson, while he was a prisoner, showing life in the castle. One of these is of the game the prisoners called *stoolball*—a form of rugby they played in their courtyard using a stool in place of the goal. Anderson made several escape attempts and abetted others. He played the oboe from a window during Pat Reid's successful escape in October 1942, stopping and starting his playing to signal where the sentries were on their beat. He also used his artistic talents as one of the camp forgers, making false identity and other documents. When the guards found his camera during a search, he made another using a lens from an old pair of glasses.

Yet somehow, despite these fascinating contents, we were mildly disappointed with the museum at Colditz. There is such a good story to tell, we were expecting to learn more about it and to see more of the place where it all happened. We thought that Colditz, like some other schlösser that we saw, was not best presented. There will soon be no survivors left from the brave, daring, and resourceful men who were prisoners of war here, and it is important that their stories are not forgotten—stories such as that of the Canadian Olympic gymnast prisoner who summersaulted over the parapet and swung from window to window to reach the ground below, the British officer who faked an ulcer and escaped from the hospital, the two Dutch prisoners who hid in the park under a camouflage net to which were sewn hundreds of leaves, and of course, those prisoners who secretly built a glider in the attic intending to launch it out of the window with a catapult. The war ended before it was finished.

The German Royal Families

On the formation of the German empire in 1871 there remained 23 German royal families who still ruled their own states. The 23 states are listed in alphabetical order below[36]. Following the abdication of Wilhelm II both as German kaiser and as king of Prussia in November 1918, all these remaining sovereigns also abdicated their powers.

In the list below the royal families who feature in this book are indicated by an asterisk*; more will be covered in my next book. Also in this book are the royal families of other ruling states that had been annexed by Prussia in the 1860s, including Hannover, Hesse-Kassel, and Nassau.

Anhalt
Baden
Bavaria
Brunswick*
Hesse-Darmstadt
Lippe
Mecklenburg-Schwerin*
Mecklenburg-Strelitz*
Oldenburg
Prussia*
Reuss-Gera
Reuss-Griez

Saxe-Altenburg
Saxe-Coburg-Gotha
Saxe-Lauenburg (later absorbed by Prussia)
Saxe-Meiningen
Saxe-Weimar-Eisenach
Saxony*
Schaumberg-Lippe
Schwarzburg-Rudolstadt
Schwartzburg-Sonderhausen
Waldeck-Pyrmont
Württemberg

Rochlitz

The last of our Saxon schlösser was Rochlitz, which is in a beautiful spot and was sparkling in the sun, high on a bluff on a bend in the river. From outside the schloss, we had a wonderful view of the lovely countryside. We could see why, like Colditz, there has been a castle here for over a thousand years. The location is close to a ford in the river and to a crossroads in the ancient trade routes.

50. The schloss at Rochlitz, in a beautiful spot on a bend in the river.

There was no information in English available at the ticket office and little on the displays, so we were pleased to find a helpful video, with a cartoon-style film and English subtitles. This showed the development of the boundaries of Saxony over the centuries under the Wettin family and the history of Rochlitz, which is similar to Colditz. The schloss was a regular Wettin residence in the Middle Ages, when rulers were in constant motion around their territory, and they later used it for hunting trips or as a dower property. Sybille (Billa), the mistress, and later the morganatic wife of Augustus the Strong's elder brother, was ennobled as the countess of Rochlitz.

Billa von Neitschutz was a precocious teenager, who packed a lot of living into her short life. She was the daughter of a pushy and ambitious mother, who was known to her contemporaries as die Generalin (the general). Born in 1675, Billa became the mistress of a Saxon courtier when she was only 12 years old, and before long she was the mistress of the heir to the Saxon throne. His father did not approve but was not very successful in keeping the lovers apart. In any event, he died in 1691, and Billa's lover became Elector Johann Georg IV.

Her mother's ambitions to advance the Neitschutz family were now looking very rosy. Johann Georg adored his mistress and showered gifts on her. But, Billa was not of royal birth, and the new elector knew that it was his duty to marry a princess and father the next heir to the throne. In 1692 he married Eleonore of Saxe-Eisenach. Not surprisingly perhaps, the marriage was not a success. It had little effect on the advance of Billa's fortunes. At Johann Georg's request she was made countess of Rochlitz, and he began lobbying to have her raised to the rank of royal princess.

In 1693, Billa and Johann Georg were morganatically married. Although he was already married to Eleonore, the elector claimed that the marriage to Billa was legal and that their children would be legitimate, even though they could not succeed to the throne. Billa and her mother may have had bigger plans. The marriage contract was backdated to 1691, which was before Johann Georg married Eleonore. If Billa were to become a princess, and therefore of equal rank to the elector, this date would make her the electress in Eleonore's place.

Billa died from smallpox in April 1694, when she was 19 years old. Her husband was devoted until the end, visiting her frequently when she was ill and sitting beside her corpse. Johann Georg caught smallpox from Billa and later in the month, he, too, died. His younger brother, Friedrich August, succeeded him and would become known as Augustus the Strong. In the aftermath of the double deaths there were many rumours and accusations of poisoning, and the finger was pointed at die Generalin. Billa's mother spent years in prison and suffered torture before she was eventually released. For the rest of her life, she wore gloves to cover the marks of the thumbscrews.

51. Commemorative plaque showing that after World War II, Rochlitz was an interrogation centre for the Soviet secret police.

During its history, Rochitz has been caught up in wars, bombarded, and besieged. But perhaps its darkest days came after World War II, when it was a centre of operations for the Soviet secret police. A modest plaque, discreetly displayed at the entrance to the schloss, records what happened there and remembers the victims. The words are in German, and my husband translated them as follows:

From 1945 to 1947, Rochlitz castle served as an operational centre for the Soviet secret police (NKWD/MWD) where prisoners were detained. After brutal interrogation, about 600 detainees were brought before the tribunal, which sentenced women, men, and young people to imprisonment or deportation to the Soviet Union. Only one third survived their years of imprisonment.

This was indeed a sombre note on which to leave the GDR. From now on, for the rest of our tour, we would be back in the old Federal Republic of Germany, or Western Germany.

6

HESSE AND
THE HOUSE OF HESSE

For the last stop on our schloss tour, we drove west to another beautiful part of Germany, to the Taunus hills, which lie to the east of the Rhine just outside Frankfurt in the state of Hesse (Hessen in German). This is a very picturesque area with rolling hills and woods. My husband and I have visited it many times over the years and find it especially beautiful in the autumn when the trees are changing colour.

Here we stayed in the Schloss Hotel Kronberg, which is one of our very favourite hotels where we have stayed a number of times over the years. The hotel is owned by the Family Foundation of the House of Hesse. In the time of the German monarchy there were three different duchies in Hesse, ruled by different branches of the Hesse family. They were the electorate of Hesse-Kassel, with its capital in Kassel; the grand duchy of Hesse-Darmstadt, with the capital in Darmstadt; and the principality of Hesse-Homburg, centred on the town of Bad Homburg. (For a brief summary of the history of the House of Hesse, please see appendix A on the royal families and main historical characters.)

Friedrichshof

Schloss Hotel Kronberg is better known to royalty buffs as Friedrichshof, the summer home built by Empress Friedrich of Prussia (Vicky) after she was widowed. She had wanted to stay in the Neues Palais in Potsdam and was then not happy with the alternatives offered instead by her son, the new kaiser, such as the Villa Leignitz in Charlottenburg (now the New Pavilion). So, with the benefit of a large legacy from a friend, she bought a villa and adjoining land in the Taunus hills. She knew the area well, as she had stayed nearby during the Franco-Prussian war of 1870. She said she loved it because it reminded her of Scotland and Balmoral, where she and Fritz had become engaged. Vicky knocked down the villa and built a new schloss to her own design. She dedicated it to her beloved Fritz. Over the entrance is still an inscription saying, 'Federici Memoriae', and the meaning of 'Friedrichshof' is, of course, 'Frederick's house'.

52. Friedrichshof is a wonderful place to stay for anyone who likes royal history.

Vicky said she wanted Friedrichshof to be a country house rather than a ceremonial palace. From a young bride, she was always vocal about the discomfort and inconvenience of living in a German schloss. So, Friedrichshof was built to the latest modern design and the highest standards of comfort. The schloss was lit by electricity, it had a lift, and there were en-suite bathrooms for the bedrooms with main drainage and hot and cold running water. And instead of being some distance away, the kitchens were located right next to the two dining rooms, so the food arrived hot to the dining table. Vicky had a reputation for being a good housewife and running her household very efficiently.

She moved into her new home in spring 1894 and spent every summer there from April or May until late in the autumn. She loved it there and felt secure that since she had paid for it with her own money, she could never be turned out by the government or her son. The house was usually full of visitors, and she enjoyed playing hostess to family and friends. There was even a degree of reconciliation with her son, Kaiser Wilhelm II. Her mother, Queen Victoria, came for the day in April 1895, when she was staying nearby in Darmstadt for the wedding of two of her grandchildren, Grand Duke Ernst Ludwig of Hesse-Darmstadt and Princess Victoria Melita of Saxe-Coburg-Gotha. The queen planted a tree in the lawn behind the schloss. It is still there today, close to others planted by Vicky's brother, King Edward VII (Bertie) and Tsar Nicholas II of Russia. Vicky was also a benefactress to the local town of Kronberg; she restored the church, built a hospital and school, and (of course) improved the drains.

Sadly, Vicky enjoyed only seven summers in her lovely new home. When her mother died in January 1901, Vicky herself was already terminally ill with cancer. Her illness was long and painful. She wrote to her daughter that the

> terrible nights of agony are worse than ever, no rest, no peace. The tears rush down my cheeks when I am not shouting with pain. The injections of morphia dull the pains a little...then

they rage again...and make me wish I were safe in my grave...
It is fearful to endure. My courage is quite exhausted.[37]

After Queen Victoria's death, Bertie (now King Edward VII) came to Friedrichshof to see his sister. Despite being outshone by her in their mother's eyes all his life, Bertie was devoted to Vicky. He was by now very worried about her state of health and tried to use the visit to arrange for her to have increased doses of morphine. She used the visit to ask his secretary, Frederick Ponsonby, to secretly smuggle her letters to her mother out of the schloss and take them back to England for safekeeping. She still remembered what had happened at the Neues Palais when her husband died.

53. Vicky towards the end of her life.

The correspondence between the queen and the empress was voluminous, as the two women had written to each other frequently since Vicky had left home as a young bride over 40 years before. Vicky's side of the correspondence would normally have been kept in England, but she had temporarily borrowed her letters back from her mother. Late at night, trusted servants delivered two large cases to Frederick Ponsonby's room. When he published the letters in 1928, he told how he had written 'China with care' on one case and 'Books with care' on the other and then waited with trepidation in the hall of Friedrichshof as the cases were carried out under the very eye of the kaiser.

The later publication of the letters caused controversy with arguments about what Vicky had intended when she entrusted them to Ponsonby and whether he should have published them. But, whatever his motives, the letters helped to show Vicky's side of the story of her relationship with her son. In her lifetime and after her death, she had a poor reputation in Germany. When I visited Frankfurt on business in the 1990s I was delighted to find that my German colleagues had a better view of her. One of them commented tellingly, 'She had a lot of trouble with her son'.

Vicky died at Friedrichshof on 5 August 1901. The weather was very hot, and her bed had been moved from her bedroom across the corridor to the atelier, or studio, which was cooler. She was a talented artist and used this room for her painting and sculpture. Today it is a small conference room. Her funeral service was held in the church in Kronberg, and she is buried at Potsdam alongside her Fritz.

She wanted Friedrichshof to continue to be lived in and to keep the contents intact, so she left it to her youngest daughter, Princess Margarethe, always known as Mossy. All of her other children had homes elsewhere, but Mossy had married into a local family. Her husband was Prince Friedrich Karl, later landgrave of Hesse-Kassel. The couple moved into Friedrichshof with their family of six sons.

Mossy's family suffered great losses during the wars. Her two eldest sons were killed in World War I, and a third, who had married a sister of

Philip Duke of Edinburgh, was killed in World War II. Two daughters-in-law also died in the second war, one in a concentration camp and the other during an air raid. Mossy's husband, Friedrich Karl, died in 1940.

Although the family were forced, for financial reasons, to leave Friedrichshof in the 1920s and move to a smaller house in the grounds, they continued to maintain the schloss, and nothing was changed. However, at the end of the World War II, it was requisitioned by the American army and used as an officers' club, and during these years it suffered a great deal of damage and pilfering. Such was the concern about what was happening at the schloss during this time that King George VI sent the royal librarian and his assistant to Friedrichshof to locate the other side of the precious correspondence between Vicky and her mother (Queen Victoria's letters to her daughter) and also bring these to England for safekeeping. The assistant in question was Anthony Blunt, who later rose to become keeper of the king's pictures and even later was revealed as having been a Soviet spy since his Cambridge days in the 1930s—the fourth man to Burgess, Maclean, and Philby!

The losses of these years included the family jewels, which had been hidden in the cellar for the duration. The hiding place was discovered and the jewels stolen. Although the culprits were found out and prosecuted, most of the jewels were never recovered. Friedrichshof was eventually restored to the family in 1953. To ensure its survival for the future, they turned it into a hotel, which opened in 1954. Mossy did not live to see the success of this venture; she never set foot inside the schloss again after it was requisitioned, and she died in January 1954.

Nearly 60 years later, the hotel is still going, and the schloss is still in the ownership of the family. It is a wonderful place to stay for anyone who likes royal history. The structure of the building and layout of the rooms are still very much as they were in Vicky's day, and some of the original contents are still there. The staff of the hotel is well aware of the building's history. A librarian from the Goethe Library in Frankfurt visits regularly to give talks about Friedrichshof and Empress

Friedrich. We heard this talk the year before when we were staying at the hotel to celebrate my retirement. And guests who are interested can get a copy from the hotel reception of a fascinating booklet about Friedrichshof and the empress, written by Roger Fulford in the 1970s. On the front cover of this is a watercolour of the schloss painted by Vicky in 1899, and on the back cover is the Winterhalter 1856 portrait of her as Princess Royal of Great Britain and Ireland. The photographs in the booklet, of the main rooms as Vicky furnished them, show that they are still recognisable today.

54. The writing table in the Kaiser Wilhelm suite is thought to be the original.

As well as the main rooms, guests can stay in bedrooms previously used by royal visitors. The suite of rooms Vicky kept for her son when he visited is now the Kaiser's suite with, we were told, the original brass bed and wonderful gilt writing table. Only Vicky's bedroom on the first floor is kept private to the family and cannot be seen by guests. Although the grounds are now a golf course, the stables are still there and also Vicky's English rose garden.

55. The Prince's Garden at Burg Kronberg.

In the old town at Kronberg, just a mile or two from Schloss Friedrichshof, is Burg Kronberg, which also belonged to Vicky. Although we have stayed in this area several times before, my husband and I had never managed to visit the burg, as it is difficult to find, either on foot or by car, and is not always open. This time, however, we were there on a weekend afternoon when it was open to the public. Entry to the museum inside the castle is by guided tour (in German), so we chose to wander around the grounds on our own with the help of a sheet of paper in English given to us at the ticket office and a helpful chat when we bumped into the guide who would later be doing the tour. It is a very pretty spot, and we particularly liked the Prince's Garden, laid out at the beginning of the 20th century and with good views of the countryside. We saw only two or three other visitors, but we were there before the first tour was due to begin.

Burg Kronberg is large and in poor repair. There are actually three castles in the grounds—the upper, middle, and lower castles. The upper castle is the oldest, built towards the end of the 12th century, and then the lower castle, built at the beginning of the 14th century and now largely disappeared. The youngest is the middle castle, built in the 14th and 15th centuries, when castles were changing from defensive fortresses to residential palaces. There was a Lord of Kronberg, but the line died out in 1704, and after that, the burg was used for a variety of purposes, including council offices, a prison, and workshops. From previous schlösser, we were already aware that once a schloss ceased to be a royal residence, there was then usually a decline into disrepair and decay.

Kaiser Wilhelm II gave Burg Kronberg to his mother, Empress Friedrich, as a Christmas present in 1891. The roofs of Friedrichshof are just visible from a certain spot in the grounds of the burg; we followed the circular trail around the upper castle to Margarethen-platzchen, or Margaret's place.

Vicky was delighted with the gift and started restoration on the middle castle. Her plan was to restore it as it would have been when the last Lord of Kronberg died and to open a museum. But she died before these plans could be carried out.

Burg Kronberg was possibly in the worst state of repair of any schloss that we saw on our tour. We enjoyed our visit and saw evidence of care, attention, and repairs. But it was clear that the burg is in need of a great deal of money to be spent on it.

Burgruine Königstein

Four miles from Kronberg, still in the Taunus hills, is another attractive small town, called Königstein. This also boasts two schlösser including one of the largest ruined castles in Germany.

56. Burgruine Königstein was dynamited by French troops in the Revolutionary Wars.

Burgruine Königstein dates from the end of the 12th century and was originally built to protect the trade route from Frankfurt to Cologne. It had a number of noble owners over the centuries but at the end of the 18th century belonged to the archbishop-elector of Mainz. The town and the castle were caught up in the French Revolutionary Wars of 1792-1802. The French twice occupied the castle and then were forced to retreat. On the second occasion in December 1796 they decided to blow it up and filled the well in the inner courtyard with gunpowder. When this exploded too early it claimed the lives of 31 French soldiers. It also blew the roofs off the castle buildings but otherwise did not do as much damage as expected.

The Three German Reichs

'Reich' is the German word for 'empire' or 'realm'. When Nazi propaganda referred to Hitler's Germany as the Third Reich it was seeking both to legitimise and to predict a glorious future for Nazi rule and also to connect it to what were portrayed as glorious epochs in Germany's past.

The First Reich was the Holy Roman Empire, when Germany consisted of hundreds of independent states whose rulers were subject to the loose authority of an elected emperor. It lasted from the early 900s until the emperor resigned, and it was disbanded during the Napoleonic Wars in 1806.

The German or Hohenzollern Empire was the Second Reich. This was formed in 1871, following victory over France in the Franco-Prussian War, when the rulers of the other German principalities invited the (Hohenzollern) king of Prussia to become kaiser (or emperor) of Germany. Although they retained their own governments and royal families, these other states then had limited sovereignty, and power was centralised, with key areas such as defence and foreign affairs being under the control of Prussia. This empire did not survive World War I; in the chaos of defeat the kaiser abdicated in November 1918, followed quickly by the other ruling princes.

The Third Reich was predicted by the Nazis to last 1000 years. In fact it lasted for only 12 years, from March 1933 when Hitler assumed dictatorial powers, until his defeat and suicide in April 1945.

Worse was to come however. In the summer of 1797 the French were back in the castle again, and this time they decided to ensure its destruction by auctioning off parts of the building. The citizens of Königstein were eager bidders at this, buying up the stone and other materials to rebuild their homes and businesses that had been destroyed by shelling from the German side during an earlier French occupation. The auction was such a success that the archbishop-elector carried out another one after the French withdrew for the third time, and he got the castle back. So, what could not be achieved by Napoleon in wartime—the destruction of Burg Königstein—was achieved by the town citizens quite peaceably. Even after the auctions they continued to take the stone secretly until this was expressly forbidden in the middle of the 19th century. The castle was never repaired and fell into ruins, as it remains today. 'Burgruine' means 'castle in ruins'.

In 1803, as part of the secularisation and mediatisation process driven by Napoleon at the end of the French Revolutionary wars, both the town and Burgruine Königstein were awarded to the dukes of Nassau as compensation for the loss of territories west of the Rhine to France. Nassau was, however, on the losing Austrian side in the Austro-Prussian War of 1866, and the duchy, with its capital in Wiesbaden, was annexed by Prussia. The reigning Duke Adolf (1817-1905) lost his principality and had to go into exile. The burgruine, however, remained in the private ownership of the Nassau family until in 1922 Duke Adolf's daughter, Hilda, gave it to the town of Königstein.

The burgruine towers over the town and is clearly visible above the rooftops. We parked the car in the High Street (Hauptstrasse) car park and walked up the steep hill through the park, as there is no parking up at the entrance. It was a sunny morning, and it was a pleasure to wander through the huge grounds inside the walls. Quite a few other visitors, including families with children, were doing the same. Although the castle is a ruin, it is very well looked after and maintained. With the help of an excellent map from the ticket office and a small booklet in English that we got beforehand from the Tourist Information office in the town, we were able to identify the various buildings and what they had been used for.

On our walk up the hill we passed Königstein's second schloss, which is also set in the park. Now called the Luxembourg Palais, this was built in the late 17th century as a summer residence for the archbishop-electors of Mainz and also came into the ownership of the Nassau family in 1803. Duke Adolf and Duchess Adelheid used it as a summer home and converted it into a grand residence in the 1870s. The widowed duchess continued to live there until her death in 1916; today it is the district court.

The present monarchies in the Netherlands and Luxembourg are of course descended from the House of Nassau. In 1890, Duke Adolf's great niece, Wilhemina, the granddaughter of his half-sister, succeeded to the Dutch throne. However, she was not able to succeed to the grand duchy of Luxembourg, although it had been linked to the Netherlands for many years, because it had the Salic law. Although only distantly related to Wilhelmina, Adolf became Grand Duke of Luxembourg under a family agreement dating back 100 years. He reigned until 1905 and was succeeded by his son, Grand Duke William IV.

Recently there was another happy link with Luxembourg when a royal wedding took place in Königstein. In September 2013 Prince Felix of Luxembourg, the second son of the current Grand Duke Henri, married Claire Lademacher in a civil ceremony in the town. Königstein was chosen as the venue for this because it was the bride's home town. A few days later the couple also had a religious ceremony in France.

57. The Luxembourg Palais was a summer residence for the house of Nassau.

Bad Homburg

To see our last schloss in the Taunus hills, we drove to the district town, Bad Homburg. Due to its proximity to Frankfurt, the town vies for the title of the wealthiest town in Germany. Frankfurt is the financial capital of Germany, and many directors and employees of the Frankfurt banks live in Bad Homburg or the surrounding area of the Taunus. The town also has a rich royal history.

Bad Homburg is famous for its mineral waters and its casino. It was these that made it a popular summer destination for European royalty at the end of the 19th century. The spa industry began in the 1830s with the discovery of the mineral waters of the Elisabethenbrunnen (Elisabeth well). The casino also dates from around the same time and is sometimes known as the Mother of Monte Carlo because it was built by the Blanc brothers, who later took over the casino in Monte Carlo. The heyday of Bad Homburg came after Kaiser Wilhelm II succeeded as German Emperor in 1888 and made the schloss an official imperial summer residence. He and his wife, Kaiserin Auguste Viktoria, were regular summer visitors. So, too, was King Edward VII, who, denied any useful occupation by his mother, devoted his time and energies to high living, and as a result had a weight problem. He came there in a vain attempt to tackle this by undergoing diet cures 32 times! Bertie also set fashion trends when he was staying in Bad Homburg with turn-ups to his trousers and the Homburg hat. The last Tsar and Tsarina were visitors, too, and in 1896 they laid the foundation stone for the Russian Orthodox chapel.

With the history of Schloss Bad Homburg, we were back to a theme with which we began our schloss tour in Celle: the story of brothers. The principality of Hesse-Homburg was created in 1622 when Duke Ludwig of Hesse-Darmstadt split his lands to give the town and district of Homburg to his younger brother, Friedrich. Friedrich I was the first landgrave and the founder of the separate line of Hesse-Homburg. He ruled until his death in 1638 and was then succeeded by three of

58. View of Schloss Bad Homburg from the Schloss Garden,
showing the White Tower.

his sons in turn. First was Wilhelm Christoph, who later sold Hesse-Homburg to his younger brother, Georg Christian. By the time Georg Christian died, the estate was mortgaged. It was left to the third brother and youngest son to save the situation (see family tree 9).

Friedrich II, known as the Prince of Homburg, was a professional soldier who lost a leg as a 26-year-old fighting for the king of Sweden and thereafter wore an artificial leg (another of his names was the Landgrave with the Silver Leg). Later he moved to Brandenburg, where he married a niece of the elector and rose to be commander of the entire Brandenburg army. After a highly successful military career, he retired to his estates in Brandenburg. On the death of his brother, however, he returned to Hesse-Homburg, where he redeemed the mortgage and then ruled as Friedrich II of Hesse-Homburg until his death in 1708. He was the builder of the baroque schloss at Bad Homburg, which replaced the medieval castle, laying the foundation stone in 1680.

The separate line of Hesse-Homburg came to an end in 1866 with the death of the last landgrave. Ferdinand was the last of five brothers, all of whom were the rulers of Hesse-Homburg in turn, and none provided an heir to continue the line. With Ferdinand's death, the sovereignty of Hesse-Homburg reverted to the Dukes of Hesse-Darmstadt but did not remain long in their possession. Later in the same year, Hesse-Darmstadt was on the losing side in the Austro-Prussian War, and Homburg was annexed by Prussia.

From then on, the schloss was owned by the Prussian royal family. Vicky stayed at Schloss Bad Homburg for some months during the Franco-Prussian War of 1870, when Fritz was away fighting. She also spent her summers at the schloss while Friedrichshof was being built. But otherwise it was not popular with the German emperors until Kaiser Wilhelm II (Willie) and Kaiserin Auguste Viktoria (Dona) used it regularly as a summer residence after he became emperor.

Bad Homburg was an especially enjoyable schloss to visit. The buildings are in very good repair, the contents are interesting, the museum attendants are really helpful, and there is a good coffee shop. I recommend a walk through the schloss park, laid out as so many of them are, as an English landscape garden. If you take the path around the lake, you will get the best views of the schloss from here.

Willie and Dona's rooms are in the King's Wing in the upper courtyard, in the middle of which is the White Tower. This is the oldest part of the schloss and predates the baroque residence of Friedrich II. But what attracted us were the charming rooms in the English Wing in the lower courtyard, which were refurbished by Landgravine Elizabeth after she was widowed. When we came to the schloss a year earlier, our visit was made special by a tour for us of the English Wing, in English, by one of the museum attendants.

59. Princess Elizabeth of Great Britain, who was happy
in her new life at Bad Homburg.

The Landgravine was born Princess Elizabeth of Great Britain, at Buckingham House in London on 22 May 1770. She was the seventh child and third daughter of King George III and Queen Charlotte, formerly Princess Sophie Charlotte of Mecklenburg-Strelitz. The British royal family was a large one, eventually growing to nine sons and six daughters. While the children were young, it was a model royal family, but as they grew older, there were tensions between parents and children, aggravated by the king's illness. His daughters did not follow the same path of a teenage marriage to a foreign prince, arranged for dynastic reasons, which we had found before with so many young princesses on our tour. Their parents did not seem at all keen to marry them off. Also during many of their marriageable years, the turmoil of the French Revolutionary Wars had an adverse effect on the European royal marriage market and the availability of suitable princes.

Untrained for any other occupations, the princesses were immensely frustrated with their spinster life at home under the close supervision of their mother, in what they called 'the nunnery'. In her early 30s, Princess Elizabeth wrote to a friend:

> I continue my prayer, "Oh, how I long to be married, be married, before that my beauty decays etc".[38]

She was not without any suitors. In her late thirties, she was hopeful of Prince Louis Philippe, the Duke of Orleans, who was then in exile in Twickenham but later became King Louis Philippe of France. But the proposal foundered on his Catholicism and Queen Charlotte's opposition. Eventually in April 1818, when she was almost 48, Elizabeth married Prince Friedrich of Hesse-Homburg, who in 1820 succeeded his father as Landgrave Friedrich VI. Friedrich was the eldest brother of Ferdinand (the last Landgrave of Hesse-Homburg) and the first of the five brothers to be the landgrave.

60. The King's Wing at Schloss Bad Homburg.

It was not a grand marriage for a princess of Great Britain and Ireland, nor was it a love match. But both bride and groom were happy with the arrangement, which brought advantages to them both. Elizabeth at last achieved the independent household for which she had so longed. Prince Friedrich acquired a well-connected and rich wife. Her dowry and annual grant from the British Parliament enabled him to remodel the schloss and made a huge difference in his tiny principality.

Respect grew into liking, and the couple became fond of each other. Elizabeth called him her 'Bluff'. When Friedrich died in 1829, she wrote,

> No woman was ever more happy than I was for eleven years, and they will often be lived over again in the memory of the heart.[39]

After his death, she refurbished her rooms in the English Wing in the style of the day. Elizabeth was an accomplished artist, and some of her work, including two lacquer panels with birds and flowers, is still on display. The rooms are elegant and comfortable, not at all as grand or elaborate as the rooms in the King's Wing, and still today reflect her personal style.

Elizabeth was happy in her life in Bad Homburg and proud of the independence she achieved late in life. She got on well with the new landgrave, who was her brother-in-law. He was a bachelor, and so she continued to play the role of landgravine and to spend her fortune in the principality. She died in 1840, aged 69. All her life, she was a great correspondent and letter writer. There is a charming 1835 portrait of her in the library of the English Wing, by Voigt, in which she is sitting at her davenport desk writing a letter. A davenport is a small desk with a sloping top. The portrait hangs above the real-life davenport desk at which she is sitting in the portrait, and on the chair hangs the real shawl that she is wearing.

The Structure of Germany Today

The Federal Republic of Germany is a parliamentary democracy with two levels of elected government—the Bundestag, which is the federal parliament in Berlin, and the Bundesrat, which are the parliaments of Germany's regional states.

The republic is made up of 16 regional states or länder. On reunification in 1990, the ten existing states of Western Germany were joined by five reconstituted states from Eastern Germany. The 16th land is the city of Berlin.

Notable by its absence from the list of Eastern states is the name of Prussia. After World War II the victorious Allies, determined not to see a resurgence of Prussian militaristic values, passed a law that the state of Prussia should never again exist.

The ten states from Western Germany (roughly north to south)
Schleswig-Holstein
Hamburg
Bremen
Lower Saxony
North Rhine-Westphalia
Hesse
Rhineland-Palatinate
Saarland
Bavaria
Baden-Württemberg

The five states from Eastern Germany (roughly north to south)
Mecklenburg-Pomerania
Brandenburg
Saxony-Anhalt
Saxony
Thuringia

7

REFLECTIONS

My husband and I agree that this was one of our best holidays ever. Visiting German schlösser turned out to be such a lot of fun. We have already done more tours, so look out for my second book (*Schloss II*) on the next 25 schlösser!

I have always had a strong interest in European royal history and found it fascinating to see the places where some of the events that I have read about took place. It gave me a more vivid picture of the historical characters and their personal stories than from just reading about these. It was not an aspect of royal history to which I had previously paid much attention. I had thought about the 'what', the 'when', and the 'who', but now I can also add the 'where'.

From visiting the museums in these schlösser, I learnt a lot about the German royal families who had owned and lived in them. The tour enabled me to connect events and people across borders, place, and time—who lived where, was related to whom, and was connected to whom by marriage. I was particularly interested in the Hanoverian succession and the later connections between the British and German royal families. And two themes emerged early in our visits that came up time and time again.

The first of these was the risks of the royal marriage market for daughters, in the only career open for most of them—a dynastic arranged marriage to a foreigner, often while still a teenager. A few, like Vicky, were winners in this lottery and had genuinely happy marriages. Others made the most of what was on offer, such as Electress Sophia or Landgravine Elizabeth. But many, despite their wealth and position, must have been deeply unhappy, and some fell by the wayside, such as Sophie Dorothee of Celle or Queen Caroline Mathilde of Denmark.

Nor was the fate of some of their brothers any more desirable. The second theme was the fate of younger sons when the only career open to them was usually that of a mercenary—to fight on the side of whoever would pay them. A few, such as the Prince of Homburg, were successful, but most were killed while they were still young, as happened with three of the six sons of Electress Sophia. We came across many stories of sibling rivalry and discord, whether this was Duke Georg Wilhelm of Celle and his younger brother, Ernst August, or Duke Johann Albrecht I of Mecklenburg-Schwerin and his younger brother, Ulrich.

My husband does not have as strong an interest in royal history as I do. However, he has done a lot of work with old buildings and was particularly interested in the schlösser from this perspective. We found that how the construction and use of these old buildings have evolved over the centuries is a very interesting study in itself. We saw how their use changed from defensive castles to royal residences intended to show off the power and the wealth of their owners and how princes designed their palaces and parks, and indeed entire towns, in imitation of the court of the French Sun King, Louis XIV. We saw how the rulers in these German principalities were often passionate builders, constantly remodelling their schlösser or building new ones, and how important their women were—both wives and mistresses—as their motivation for building.

We saw, too, how the abdication of the princes after World War I and the confiscation of their property started a decline in the fortunes of many schlösser, particularly for those that would be behind the Iron Curtain for nearly 50 years. But this is a relatively short period in the life of these old buildings, and it was heartening to see that many are now under renovation and again open as museums. In a prince's time, a schloss served several purposes: it was his residence where he held court and entertained guests but also the seat of government from which he administered his lands. It seemed to us that the schlösser that had fared best in the current time and were in best repair were those being used in a way that was close to their original purpose—for example, Friedrichshof as a hotel and Schwerin as the home of the state parliament.

Our experience when we visited these schlösser was, of course, entirely personal and may not be representative of every foreign visitor. However, after visiting 25 in a relatively short time, we felt we could almost write a book for museum staff on the dos and don'ts from the perspective of the visitor. Some of our advice would be fairly basic. For example: do have lots of signs making it clear where to park and how to get to the schloss. On too many occasions, we could not find our way either by car or on foot because of the lack of signs, and we had to ask for directions. Another suggestion would be to abolish the need for a photo permit in those schlösser that still require them.

Other advice would be about the experience of walking around the museum and looking at the exhibits. The mandatory tour with a real or audio guide is not always best for the visitors, who may hear only a rehearsed patter and have no time to explore what interests them. Many visitors prefer to wander at their own speed and want good visual material to read and charts and pictures to look at. Most importantly, the exhibits need to tell a story and bring the history of the schloss to life rather than just recount extensive historical detail. Also, if the schloss wants to attract foreign visitors, the material needs to be translated. Great examples of curating that we saw on our tour included the story of the four dukes of Brunswick-Lüneburg at Celle Castle and the internal room with the genealogy of the Wettin Kings of Saxony at Pillnitz. Oh, and by the way, as visitors, we did appreciate it when the schloss had a good coffee shop.

But if we had to pick out one thing as the most important piece of feedback, we would say it is the approach of the museum attendants. The visitors' experience depends more on this than on any other factor, more than whether the schloss is smart or shabby or how the exhibits are laid out. In some places, we were made to feel like interlopers on their territory who must be herded about and controlled. Fortunately, in others we were treated as we should be—as customers who were welcomed and helped to enjoy their visit.

The Author's Favourite Schlösser

Ludwigslust in Mecklenburg-Pomerania
Celle Castle in Lower Saxony
Pillnitz in Saxony
Paretz in Brandenburg
Friedrichshof in Hesse

From the 25 that we saw, we, of course, had some favourites. Celle, the first that we visited, was for us the best curated. The exhibits were interesting and attractively laid out, making us want to find out about the events and the story they told. Other schlösser also did this well, but none quite came up to Celle standard. We loved three others, too: Pillnitz for the sheer beauty of the site and the design of buildings and gardens as the king's pleasure palace; Paretz as the country idyll and model play farm of a royal couple in love; and Friedrichshof as the realisation of Vicky's talents and where she found some contentment. But our overall favourite must be Ludwigslust, the exuberant palace built on a grand scale by a pious and frugal duke, which later fell on hard times, the *Sleeping Beauty* palace that is now coming back to life.

We would recommend to anyone visiting Germany that they take time to visit some of the schlösser. While there are some that are well known and busy, there are others that have too few visitors. In our view, these German schlösser are undermarketed, and we hope this book will help to show what attractive places they are to visit. And if you do make a visit to any of the schlösser included, I hope that reading this book and knowing more about their history will enhance your experience.

Marksburg and the German Castles Association

High above the small town of Braubach on the right bank of the Rhine, on a bend in the river, towers majestic Marksburg Castle. Built on a steep wooded hill, it commands a long stretch of the Rhine. The castle is so tall that some walls need to be three metres thick, just to support the weight of the structure. Dating mainly from the 13th and 15th centuries this is the only surviving Rhine castle that has never been destroyed or remodelled. The only serious

damage it ever suffered was in 1945 when it was shelled from the left bank by the advancing American army. In its time Marksburg has belonged to several noble German families, including the houses of Hesse and Nassau. Today it belongs to, and is the home of, the German Castles Association.

This members association dates from 1899 and was founded by Professor Bodo Ebhart, architect and castle enthusiast. In 1900, with the help of Kaiser Wilhelm II, he acquired Schloss Marksburg and carried out extensive restoration. He lived in Marksburg until his death in 1945 and is buried there. The association also now owns *Schloss Philippsburg*, down the hill in the centre of Braubach, which holds their unique library of 30,000 books on castles. Everyone can join the association; its aim is the preservation and enjoyment of this important part of Germany's cultural heritage. It sponsors research and publishes a journal; understandably, all its publications are in German.

Marksburg is open to the public and is well worth a visit. Visitors climb up the Riders staircase, hewn out of solid rock, where in medieval times the knights in armour rode their horses to the stables above. The castle shows life as it was in the late Middle Ages, including the great hall, kitchen, wine cellars, herb garden, a smithy, weaving room, and even the dog kennel. My favourite was the Ladies Bower at the top of the castle with a window seat set into the thickness of the walls. Here the noble ladies could sit, talk, and spin with a magnificent view of the river below. I also enjoyed the armoury with a display of life-sized models in soldier's outfits, ranging in time from a Greek warrior of 600BC and a Roman legionnaire of 100AD to a knight of the 15th century and a 17th-century musketeer.

For more information on the German Castles Association visit www. marksburg.de (also available in English).

APPENDICES

Appendix A: The Royal Families and Main Historical Characters

Brunswick

The House of Brunswick with the family name of Guelph or Welf dates back to at least the 12th century and their famous forbear Henry the Lion. By the 17th century the house was divided into the lines of Brunswick-Lüneburg and Brunswick-Wolfenbüttel. The first of these is featured in this book, the second is in my next book, *Schloss II*.

The Brunswick-Lüneburg line held the dukedoms of Celle and Calenberg. It became the House of Hannover when Duke Ernst August of Calenberg was created elector of Hannover in 1692. The electors of Hannover also became kings of Great Britain in 1714, when Elector Georg Ludwig (the son of Duke Ernst August) succeeded his distant kinswoman, Queen Anne, and became George I. From then until 1837 (when Queen Victoria succeeded) all British monarchs were also electors and later kings of Hannover (Hannover became a kingdom in 1814).

Under Hanoverian law, Victoria was not able to succeed in Hannover (because she was not male), so, her uncle, the duke of Cumberland, became king of Hannover in 1837. Victoria was the last Hanoverian monarch of Great Britain. When she married Prince Albert in 1840, the family name of the British monarchy became Saxe-Coburg-Gotha in place of Guelph.

Hannover continued as a separate kingdom until 1866 when it was annexed by Prussia and the last king, George V, was deposed. But King George and his son refused to renounce their rights to the kingdom until 1913, when his grandson married the great-granddaughter of his enemy, the king of Prussia. They remained dukes of Cumberland and princes of Great Britain and Ireland until 1915 when they were stripped of all their British titles during World War I.

The principality of Brunswick-Wolfenbüttel became the duchy of Brunswick in 1815, after the Napoleonic Wars. The Brunswick-

Wolfenbüttel line died out in 1884, with the death of the last duke, William VIII. The duchy of Brunswick should then have passed to the Brunswick-Lüneburg line, but this was prevented by Prussia because of their intransigence over their Hanoverian rights. It was eventually agreed that Ernst August III, the grandson of George V, should become duke of Brunswick when he married the Prussian princess, Viktoria Luise, in 1913. However, he was not duke for long, abdicating his rights, along with the other ruling German princes after World War I, in 1918.

The current head of the house of Brunswick-Lüneburg is Ernst August V, born in 1954.

Georg, Duke of Calenberg was one of six brothers and is known as the Marrying Duke because he successfully drew lots with his brothers to be the one who would marry and carry on the line. He had four sons, who are known as the Four Dukes of Brunswick-Lüneburg.

Georg Wilhelm, Duke of Celle was the second eldest of the four sons of George, Duke of Calenberg. He remodelled *Celle Castle* and held court there. He caused tension in the family when he fell in love and married outside the royal circle.

Eleonore d'Olbreuse was a French noblewoman who married Duke Georg Wilhelm of Celle. Because she was not of royal birth, the marriage was not recognised by his family. She campaigned successfully for her rights to be recognised as duchess but unsuccessfully for the release of Sophie Dorothee, her imprisoned daughter.

Ernst August, Elector of Hannover was the youngest of the four dukes of Brunswick-Lüneburg and the founder of the House of Hannover. He had a spectacular rise in life from landless younger son to one of the eight electors of the Holy Roman Empire and ancestor of the kings of Great Britain, Prussia, Denmark, and Hannover.

Sophia, Electress of Hannover. Although engaged first to his elder brother, Sophia married Ernst August, duke of Brunswick-Lüneburg and later elector of Hannover. She was born the 12th child of a deposed king, but her amazing life story saw her rise to become heiress to the throne of Great Britain. She was the creator of the gardens at *Herrenhausen*.

Sophie Dorothee, Princess of Celle was the only child of Duke Georg Wilhelm of Celle and Eleonore d'Olbreuse and was unhappily married to Georg Ludwig of Hannover before he became King George I of Britain. When her affair with an army officer was discovered she was separated from her children and banished for life to the schloss at *Ahlden*.

George I, King of Great Britain and Elector of Hannover was born Georg Ludwig of Hannover, the son of Elector Ernst August and Electress Sophia. He inherited his mother's position as heir to Great Britain and succeeded Queen Anne. He always much preferred Hannover to his new kingdom and is buried at *Herrenhausen*.

Sophie Charlotte, Princess of Hannover was the daughter of Elector Ernst August and Electress Sophia and known as Figuelotte in the family. She married King Friedrich I of Prussia as his second wife. When she died young, her husband named *Charlottenburg* in her memory. She was the grandmother of Frederick the Great.

George III, King of Great Britain and Elector of Hannover was the first of the dynasty to be born in Britain and speak English as his first language. He succeeded his grandfather (George II) aged 22 and reigned for nearly 60 years. He married Sophie Charlotte of Mecklenburg-Strelitz. He suffered from bouts of what was diagnosed as madness but is now thought likely to have been a rare blood disorder called porphyria. He spent his last years alone, blind, and shut away.

Caroline Mathilde, Queen of Denmark and Norway, was the sister of George III and was married young to the mentally unbalanced king of Denmark. She fell in love with and became the mistress of the king's doctor, who also became his first minister. In a palace coup, both were arrested. She was divorced and exiled from Denmark finding refuge at her brother's castle in *Celle*; she died there from scarlet fever, aged only 23. The doctor, Johann Struensee was executed.

Ernst August I, Duke of Cumberland and King of Hannover was the fifth son of George III. He was a hated figure in Britain, suspected of heinous crimes, including incest and murder. He became king of Hannover when Victoria succeeded, and the thrones of Britain and Hannover were split. He married Friederike of Mecklenburg-Strelitz.

Victoria, Queen of Great Britain and Ireland was the longest reigning British monarch until Queen Elizabeth II overtook her in September 2015. Victoria came to the throne as an 18-year-old and died at 82 as the monarch of an empire on which the sun never set. Fiercely protective of her rights as the sovereign of a great power, she ruled her family with a rod of iron. Her children and grandchildren married into most of Europe's royal families. She was the last British monarch from the house of Hannover.

George V, King of Hannover was the son of King Ernst August I and Queen Friederike and was blind from childhood. He was heir to his cousin, Queen Victoria of Great Britain and Ireland, until she married and had children. If Victoria had died young, George would also have been king of Great Britain. The last king of Hannover, he was deposed when Hannover was annexed by Prussia. He was the builder of *Marienburg*.

Ernst August III, Duke of Brunswick was the grandson of George V of Hannover. He became the last reigning duke of Brunswick on his marriage to Viktoria Luise of Prussia and abdicated at the end of World War I. In 1945 the couple fled to *Marienburg* in the British zone of occupation and lived there until the duke's death.

Viktoria Luise, Duchess of Brunswick and Princess of Prussia was the only daughter of Kaiser Wilhelm II. Her marriage in 1913 was the last great gathering of European royalty before the calamity of World War I, following which many of them lost their thrones.

Mecklenburg

The Mecklenburg family is another ancient German royal house that dates back to the 12th century. The founder of the house, Niklot, was a prince of the Slavonic tribe of Obodrites. His son, Pribislaw, converted to Christianity and was made a prince of the Holy Roman Empire.

Due to the practice of spitting the family inheritance between sons, there were various divisions of land in the history of the house. Mecklenburg-Güstrow was created as a separate principality for a younger brother of Johann Albrecht I in the 16th century but died out and reverted to the senior line after about 150 years. In the early 18th century there was another split, with Duke Friedrich Wilhelm becoming the ruler of Mecklenburg-Schwerin and his uncle, Duke Adolphus Friedrich II, of the much smaller Mecklenburg-Strelitz. Characters from both these lines are included in this book. Following the division both duchies descended by primogeniture. In 1815 at the Congress of Vienna, which reset European boundaries at the end of the Napoleonic Wars, the rulers of both were elevated to the title of grand duke.

The present day Dutch royal family is descended from the house of Mecklenburg-Schwerin. In 1901 Duke Henry of Mecklenburg-Schwerin, the youngest brother of ruling Duke Friedrich Franz III, married Queen Wilhelmina of the Netherlands. Wilhelm-Alexander, who became king in 2013, is his great-grandson.

The rule of the Mecklenburg-Strelitz line came to an end in early 1918 with the suicide of the last grand duke, Adolphus Friedrich VI. Later that year, at the close of World War I, Grand Duke Friedrich Franz IV of Mecklenburg-Schwerin abdicated on behalf of both duchies.

Both Mecklenburg lines continue to the present day. The head of the house of Mecklenburg-Schwerin is currently Duchess Donata, born in 1956. Her distant cousin, Duke Borwin, born the same year, is head of the house of Mecklenburg-Strelitz.

Mecklenburg-Schwerin

Johann Albrecht I, Duke of Mecklenburg-Schwerin was the reigning duke when the family lands were split following arbitration on a family dispute, and the separate dukedom of Mecklenburg-Güstrow was created. He transformed *Schwerin* from a defensive fortress into a princely residence.

Ulrich, Duke of Mecklenburg-Güstrow was the brother of Johann Albrecht I and became the first duke of the line of Mecklenburg-Güstrow when the lands were split. Not to be outdone by his brother, he also did extensive building work on his castle at *Güstrow.*

Friedrich II, Duke of Mecklenburg-Schwerin was an eccentric character who banned cards and dancing and was known as Friedrich the Pious. He built *Ludwigslust* and moved his residence there. He was also the driving force behind the local industry of 'Ludwigslust carton' and the use of papier-mâché as a building material.

Friedrich Franz I, Grand Duke of Mecklenburg-Schwerin succeeded his uncle, Friedrich II, and also reigned from *Ludwigslust.* He had a summer home at *Bad Doberan* and founded the seaside spa resort at Heiligendamm.

Helena Paulowna, Grand Duchess of Russia was one of the six daughters of Tsar Paul I and was married as a teenager to the son and heir of Friedrich Franz I. She died young from consumption and is buried in the mausoleum at *Ludwigslust.* Her son, Grand Duke Paul Friedrich, succeeded his grandfather and moved the centre of the duchy back to *Schwerin.*

Friedrich Franz III, Grand Duke of Mecklenburg-Schwerin was the grandson of Paul Friedrich. He suffered from ill health and was criticised for spending many months each year away from the duchy, in a warmer climate. When he did visit he preferred to stay away from the capital in his hunting lodge at *Gelbensande.* He died in the south of France, possibly by suicide, while still in his forties.

Anastasia Mikhailowna, grand duchess of Russia (always known as Stassie), was the wife of Friedrich Franz III and the mother of Crown Princess Cecilie of Prussia. Stassie's scandalous lifestyle after her husband's early death resulted in her being banned from visiting her daughter in Berlin. As a widow, Stassie rarely returned to Mecklenburg; when she did, she often stayed at *Gelbensande.*

Johann Albrecht, Duke of Mecklenburg-Schwerin was the brother of Friedrich Franz III and, after his early death, the regent for his brother's minor son, Friedrich Franz IV. He built *Wiligrad* for his first wife.

Cecilie, Princess of Mecklenburg-Schwerin was the daughter of Friedrich Franz III and married the crown prince of Prussia. They got engaged at *Gelbensande* and built *Cecilienhof* during World War I as their summer home. But the couple never became king and queen as the Prussian monarchy was abolished at the end of the war. She was the only senior member of the royal family to stay on in Germany.

Friedrich Franz IV was the brother of Cecilie and succeeded his father aged only 15. He was the last grand duke of Mecklenburg-Schwerin, abdicating in 1918.

Mecklenburg-Strelitz

Sophie Charlotte, Princess of Mecklenburg-Strelitz became a big winner in the marriage market when she married George III of Great Britain. She was queen consort of Great Britain for 57 years and the mother of 15 children. She became estranged from her husband in later years, following his illness, and was a difficult old woman.

Luise, Princess of Mecklenburg-Strelitz was the daughter of Queen Charlotte's brother and was also a success in the marriage market. She married Friedrich Wilhelm III to become the most famous and best-loved queen of Prussia. Her life was not always easy; after Napoleon invaded her attempt to intercede with him on behalf of her adopted country is part of her legend. She suffered from heart disease, died young, and is buried in the mausoleum at *Charlottenburg*.

Friederike, Princess of Mecklenburg-Strelitz was the younger sister of Luise and when Luise married Friedrich Wilhelm III of Prussia, Friederike married his younger brother. She was widowed young, and her subsequent marital history scandalised society. Her third marriage, to Ernest, Duke of Cumberland, was the most successful. She was the mother of George V of Hannover.

Hohenzollern

The House of Hohenzollern originally takes its name from the family's ancestral seat, Schloss Hohenzollern, which is near Stuttgart in the south German state of Baden-Württemberg. In the 12th century the family split into two—the Hohenzollern (which is featured in this book) and the less well known Hohenzollern-Sigmaringen branch.

The Hohenzollern-Sigmaringen branch was Catholic and the senior of the two lines. They ruled as lords of Sigmaringen until deposed in 1848 (the year of European revolutions), and in 1850 their lands were annexed by Prussia. In 1866 Prince Karl of Hohenzollern-Sigmaringen became prince and later King Carol of Romania. His family ruled until 1947 when his great-great-nephew, King Michael (born in 1921), was forced to abdicate by the communist regime. After the fall of communism Michael returned to Romania and now lives there part time. His heir is his eldest daughter, Princess Margareta.

The junior Hohenzollern branch became Protestant and were Burgraves of Nuremburg until in 1417 they purchased the Mark of Brandenburg from the Holy Roman emperor and moved north to become electors of Brandenburg. Brandenburg was a frontier province of the Holy Roman Empire and relatively poor, but under the Hohenzollerns it would become the heartland of the kingdom of Prussia and ultimately of the German Empire. Here they would found their great capital of Berlin.

Two hundred years later the Hohenzollern acquired the second major part of their lands when the duchy of Prussia passed to them in 1618 on marriage. The duchy had previously been ruled by the Teutonic order of Knights from their castle at Königsberg. In 1701, with the consent of the Holy Roman emperor, Elector Friedrich III of Brandenburg crowned himself King Friedrich I in Prussia, and thereafter this became the family's senior title.

Prussia was not adjacent to, but separated from, Brandenburg by part of Poland. Prussia acquired further detached territory under the

1815 Treaty of Vienna at the end of the Napoleonic Wars, including wealthy cities on the Rhine, such as Koblenz and Cologne, and the Ruhr valley, which would provide its industrial base. Prussia was now recognised as one of the great powers in Europe and would vie with Austria for the leadership of Germany.

In 1861 King Wilhelm succeeded his brother as king of Prussia, and the following year he appointed Bismarck as his chief minister. Over the next ten years Bismarck would follow what he called a policy of 'blood and iron' to forge a united Germany. In 1863 Prussia and Austria defeated Denmark in the war over the duchies of Schleswig and Holstein, and Prussia gained access to the Baltic and the important port of Kiel. In 1866 Prussia turned on her previous ally and defeated Austria in the Seven Weeks' War. The north German states that had sided with Austria, such as Hannover, Hesse-Kassel, and Nassau, were annexed, and Prussia was joined to her previously detached territory on the Rhine. In another swift campaign, Prussia defeated France in the Franco-Prussian War of 1870, and the French provinces of Alsace and Lorraine were also annexed. In January 1871, King Wilhelm of Prussia was declared kaiser of a united German Empire in the Hall of Mirrors at Versailles.

The great conflict of World War I led to the downfall of the German Empire. In November 1918, Kaiser Wilhelm II (the grandson of the first kaiser), abdicated as German emperor and king of Prussia and lived the rest of his life in exile in Holland.

The present head of the House of Hohenzollern is his great-great-grandson, Georg Friedrich, born in 1976.

Friedrich I, King in Prussia was previously Elector Friedrich III of Brandenburg and crowned himself the first king in Prussia in Königsberg in January 1701. He married Sophie Charlotte of Hannover as his second wife and was the father of Friedrich Wilhelm I.

Friedrich Wilhelm I, King in Prussia was a difficult man to live with and a martinet who inflicted brutal punishments on his son. Known as the

'Soldier King' he reformed the army and the civil service and helped turn Prussia into a centralised and absolutist state. He was famous for building up a mercenary regiment of very tall soldiers, whom he often purchased or kidnapped from abroad. He was married to Sophie Dorothee of Hannover and was the father of Frederick the Great.

Friedrich II, King of Prussia was the most famous king of Prussia, known as Frederick the Great. He suffered as a young man at the hands of his father, who was determined to turn him into his idea of a model Prussian prince. He became a talented and successful general, of whom his father would have been proud, but was also interested in the arts and the patron of Voltaire. He separated from his wife as soon as he had the freedom to do so and was succeeded by his nephew. He was the builder of *Sanssouci* and also the *Neues Palais*.

Friedrich Wilhelm II, King of Prussia was the nephew and successor of Frederick the Great and a complete contrast to his uncle. Little interested in the business of government he preferred more pleasurable pursuits. His private life was colourful; in addition to two dynastic marriages, the first of which ended in divorce, he made two bigamistic morganatic marriages and had a longstanding mistress.

Friedrich Wilhelm III, King of Prussia was the son of Friedrich Wilhelm II and his second wife and had a lonely childhood that affected his character. A diffident and hesitant man, he relied heavily on his wife, Queen Luise. He suffered a heavy defeat at the hands of Napoleon in the Battles of Jena-Auerstadt and had to flee his kingdom. He was happiest with Luise in the country at *Paretz*, which he turned into a model farming community. He did not marry again until many years after her death, when he made a morganatic marriage to Princess Leignitz and built the *New Pavilion* for his second wife.

Wilhelm I, Emperor of Germany was the son of Friedrich Wilhelm III and Queen Luise and succeeded his brother, Friedrich Wilhelm IV. He appointed Bismarck as his first minister and supported his policy of 'blood and iron'. He became the first emperor of a united Germany, following Prussia's victory in the Franco-Prussian War.

Friedrich III, Emperor of Germany (Fritz) was the only son of Wilhelm I. He was happily married to Vicky, the eldest child of Queen Victoria, and influenced by her liberal views. A fine general, he was however marginalised by the ruling Prussian clique because of his liberal views. Fritz was a disappointed man, who was already dying when he came to the throne and could not put through his planned reforms. Together with Vicky he renovated the *Neues Palais.*

Wilhelm II, Emperor of Germany was the son of Vicky and Fritz. He did not get on with his parents and behaved badly to his mother when his father died. Later he made some amends and gave her *Burg Kronberg* as a Christmas present. A complex and arrogant man, he referred to himself as the 'All-Highest'. Known as Kaiser Bill in World War I, he abdicated in 1918, and the monarchy was abolished. He lived out his life in exile in Holland.

Wilhelm, Crown Prince of Prussia was the eldest son of Wilhelm II and heir to the Prussian throne. With his wife, Cecilie, he built *Cecilienhof* during World War I. He was exiled from Germany at the end of the war, when the monarchy was abolished.

Wettin

The house of Wettin can trace its ancestry back to the 10th century and earlier. They were originally Margraves of Meissen and in 1423 were made electors of Saxony by the Holy Roman emperor. From then on the family took this as their senior title.

Like the other ancient houses, the Wettin were prone to division, and in 1485 there was a lasting split when the brothers, Ernest and Albert, split the house and its lands into two branches called the Ernestine and the Albertine. Ernest was the elder brother and retained the electorate but, after various vicissitudes, his descendants were forced to cede this to his brother's descendants. Thereafter the Ernestine line was less important than the Albertine. The Ernestine branch went through further divisions and from this line were descended several royal families including that of Saxe-Coburg-Gotha. This book features the electorate of Saxony (Albertine line) and some royal characters from the duchy of Saxe-Coburg-Gotha (Ernestine line).

On the 1485 split, the junior Albertine branch of the Wettins took the margraviate of Meissen, although (as above), they later acquired the electorate of Saxony from the Ernestine branch. While Saxony was a protestant state, the Albertine branch of the Wettin family were catholic following the conversion of Elector Friedrich August I (Augustus the Strong), made in order to qualify for election to the Polish throne. He was king of Poland, as well as elector of Saxony from 1697 until his death in 1733, with an interregnum between 1706 and 1709.

In 1806 Elector Friedrich August III (the great-grandson of Augustus the Strong) suffered a crushing defeat alongside Prussia at the battles of Jena-Auerstadt; he then made a separate peace with Napoleon and was rewarded by being promoted from elector and made the first king of Saxony as Friedrich August I.

Friedrich August III was the last king of Saxony; like the other ruling German princes, he abdicated in 1918. The current head of the Royal House of Saxony is Prince Alexander, born in 1954.

The duchy of Saxe-Coburg-Gotha came into being on the reorganisation in 1826 of various Ernestine lands, when Duke Ernst III of Saxe-Coburg-Saalfeld became Ernst I of Saxe-Coburg-Gotha. It was a small German principality, but the ruling family gained prominence during the 19th century due to their successful marriage policy. In a famous quote, Chancellor Bismarck said Coburg was 'the stud farm of Europe'. In 1831 the brother of Ernst I was elected King Leopold I of a newly independent Belgium, and the present King Philippe of Belgium is his great-great-great-grandson. A few years later in 1836 the son of another brother, Ferdinand, married Queen Maria II da Gloria and became king consort of Portugal. King Manoel, the last king before the Portuguese monarchy was abolished in 1910, was their great-grandson.

And in 1837, Ernst I's niece (the daughter of his sister Victoire) succeeded as Queen Victoria of Great Britain and Ireland; in 1840 she would marry his younger son, Albert. Queen Elizabeth II is their great-great-granddaughter. The surname of British monarchs was Saxe-Coburg until 1917 when King George V changed it to Windsor for fear of being thought too German.

Ernst I was succeeded by his elder son; Ernst II was, however, childless, and on his death in 1893 he was succeeded by Victoria and Albert's second son, Alfred. Alfred's only son predeceased him, so, on his death in 1900, he was succeeded by his nephew Karl Eduard, who was the son of Queen Victoria's youngest son, Leopold. Karl Eduard was the last duke of Saxe-Coburg-Gotha.

Saxony

Elector Johann Georg IV was the elder brother of Augustus the Strong; he died young of smallpox so that Augustus unexpectedly came to the throne.

Sybille, Countess of Rochlitz, (Billa) was the child of a pushy and ambitious mother, and she became the mistress of Elector Johann Georg IV while still a teenager. She was ennobled as the Countess of *Rochlitz* but died of smallpox, which she passed onto Johann Georg.

Friedrich August I, Elector of Saxony, also Augustus II, King of Poland was known as Augustus the Strong, and he is the most famous Saxon monarch and the founder of baroque Dresden. Augustus lived a lavish lifestyle and had a string of mistresses, including Countess Cosel, for whom he built the *Taschenbergpalais*. He also built the pleasure palace at *Pillnitz*.

Anna Constantia, Countess Cosel was beautiful and ambitious and became the mistress of Augustus the Strong, elector of Saxony. When she fell from favour she tried to blackmail him and was imprisoned in the fortress at *Stolpen* for 49 years until her death.

Friedrich August I, King of Saxony (previously Elector Friedrich August III) was the great-grandson of Augustus the Strong, and succeeded as a child and was the longest reigning ruler of Saxony. Known as Friedrich the Just, he was elector at the time of the French wars. A keen botanist, he extended the gardens at *Pillnitz* and built up a botanical nursery there.

Georg, King of Saxony succeeded his brother in 1902 aged nearly 70 and reigned until his death two years later. He was the father-in-law of Crown Princess Luise and his short reign was overshadowed by the scandal of his daughter-in-law's flight.

Luise, Crown Princess of Saxony was born an archduchess of Hapsburg-Tuscany, and she became crown princess of Saxony and lived in the *Taschenbergpalais*. When her father-in-law threatened to have her committed to a lunatic asylum, she ran away to Switzerland with her children's tutor. Her story was heavily covered by the world's press. She never saw her children again.

Friedrich August III, King of Saxony was the son of King Georg and husband of Crown Princess Luise. He was the last king of Saxony and abdicated in 1918. He never married again after his divorce from Luise.

Saxe-Coburg-Gotha

Albert, Prince Consort of Great Britain was the second son of Ernst I of Saxe-Coburg-Gotha, and married his cousin Queen Victoria. Despite the complete difference in their characters, the marriage was a success, and the queen was plunged into despair and grief on his early death. He supported Prussia for the leadership of Germany and imagined a great destiny for his eldest child as empress of Germany. This was not to be.

Victoria, Empress of Prussia (Vicky) was the eldest child of Queen Victoria and Prince Albert. She married Emperor Friedrich III of Germany and lived in the *Altes Palais* as a new bride. She was a spiky character who was always unpopular in her adopted country. Vicky had a bad relationship with her son, Emperor Wilhelm II. As a widow, she found some contentment in building her own summer home at *Friedrichshof.*

Edward VII, King of Great Britain and Ireland (Bertie) was the second child and eldest son of Queen Victoria and Prince Albert. He was devoted to his sister, Vicky, despite being always overshadowed by her in their parents' eyes and visited her at *Friedrichshof* before she died. He helped to make *Bad Homburg* a fashionable summer resort town.

Hesse

The principality of Hesse was created in the 13ᵗʰ century when a younger son of the Duke of Brabant became Landgrave Henry I of Hesse. In 1567, on the death of Landgrave Philip the Magnanimous, there was a division of lands between his sons, and two lasting branches of the House of Hesse were founded—the lines of Hesse-Kassel and Hesse-Darmstadt.

Wilhelm IV was the first landgrave of Hesse-Kassel, which was the senior of the two lines. In 1803 Landgrave Wilhelm IX was elevated in status to become Elector Wilhelm I, but in the same year his principality was annexed by Napoleon to become part of the new kingdom of Westphalia (ruled by Napoleon's brother, Jerome). It was not restored until 1813. Wilhelm I hoped to be made a king by the Congress of Vienna at the end of the Napoleonic Wars; when this did not come about, he and his descendants continued to use the title of elector even though the Holy Roman Empire had been dissolved in 1806.

The last elector was his grandson, Friedrich Wilhelm I, who was on the losing side in the Austro-Prussian War of 1866 and saw his principality annexed by Prussia. After his death in 1875 the succession passed to cousins, who reverted to using the title of landgrave. Friedrich Wilhelm I had made a morganatic marriage so his own children were not eligible to succeed him; instead they were given the title of princes of Hanau.

Prince Friedrich Karl, the husband of Mossy (Princess Margarethe of Prussia, the daughter of Vicky), became landgrave of Hesse in 1925, after the abdication of his elder brother. The current head of house is Landgrave Donatus, born in 1966. He is the great-grandson of Landgrave Friedrich Karl and Mossy.

Georg I became the first landgrave of Hesse-Darmstadt on the split in 1567. In the next century there was a further division when in 1622 Ludwig V split Hesse-Darmstadt to create the small principality of Hesse-Homburg for his younger brother, Friedrich I. Hesse-Homburg, which is featured in this book, continued as a separate line until 1866 when it became extinct and reverted back to Hesse-Darmstadt. In the same year, however, Hesse-Darmstadt was on the losing side in the Austro-Prussian War and Hesse-Homburg was annexed by Prussia.

In 1806, Landgrave Ludwig IX of Hesse-Darmstadt gained the more prestigious title of Grand Duke Ludwig I as part of the shake up and reorganisation of states on the breakup of the Holy Roman Empire. This increase in status was recognised by the Congress of Vienna, but his title was then changed to grand duke of Hesse and by Rhine. It later changed back to Hesse-Darmstadt.

The last grand duke of Hesse-Darmstadt was Ernst Ludwig (Ernie), whose mother was Princess Alice of Great Britain, the second daughter of Queen Victoria. He abdicated at the end of World War I along with the other ruling German princes and died in October 1937. Just weeks later his eldest son, Georg Donatus, was killed in a tragic plane crash with his wife and two young sons. They had been on their way to the wedding of Ernie's younger son, Ludwig, in London. Ludwig and his new wife adopted the baby daughter who had been left at home, but sadly she died of meningitis before she was three.

When Ludwig died childless in 1968, the succession passed by family agreement to the senior Hesse-Kassel branch. As above, the current head of the house is Landgrave Donatus.

Hesse-Kassel

Margarethe, Landgravine of Hesse was the daughter of Vicky and known in the family as Mossy. She inherited *Friedrichshof* from her mother. She married Landgrave Friedrich Karl of Hesse-Kassel and had six sons. The family suffered great losses of life and property in the two World Wars.

Hesse-Homburg

Friedrich II, Landgrave of Hesse-Homburg was a successful mercenary who lost a leg fighting and was known as the Landgrave with the Silver Leg. When he succeeded his brother as Landgrave later in life, he redeemed the mortgage on the principality and built schloss *Bad Homburg.*

Elizabeth, Landgravine of Hesse-Homburg was the daughter of King George III and Queen Charlotte of Great Britain. Desperate to marry, she did not find a husband until she was 47, when she married Friedrich VII of Hesse-Homburg and lived at *Bad Homburg.* Surprisingly the marriage was a success; Elizabeth found happiness and independence in her new life.

**Appendix B: Simplified Family Trees for Some of the
Historical Characters**

1. The four dukes of Brunswick-Lüneburg and the succession to the throne of Great Britain.
2. The separation of the kingdoms of Hannover and Great Britain.
3. The dukes of Mecklenburg-Schwerin and the builders of Ludwigslust.
4. The line of Mecklenburg-Strelitz and their royal brides.
5. The ancestry of Frederick the Great of Prussia.
6. The descendants of Friedrich Wilhelm III and Queen Luise.
7. Augustus the Strong and Countess Cosel.
8. The marriages of Luise, Crown Princess of Saxony.
9. The 12 landgraves of Hesse-Homburg.

1. THE FOUR DUKES OF BRUNSWICK-LÜNEBURG AND THE SUCCESSION TO THE THRONE OF GREAT BRITAIN

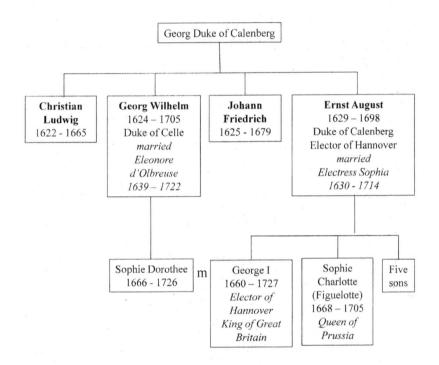

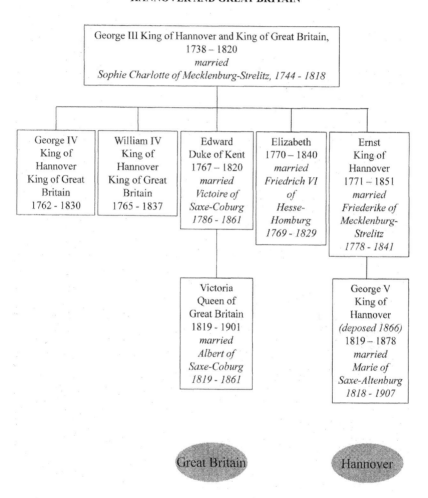

2. THE SEPARATION OF THE KINGDOMS OF HANNOVER AND GREAT BRITAIN

George III King of Hannover and King of Great Britain, 1738 – 1820
married
Sophie Charlotte of Mecklenburg-Strelitz, 1744 - 1818

| George IV King of Hannover King of Great Britain 1762 - 1830 | William IV King of Hannover King of Great Britain 1765 - 1837 | Edward Duke of Kent 1767 – 1820 *married Victoire of Saxe-Coburg 1786 - 1861* | Elizabeth 1770 – 1840 *married Friedrich VI of Hesse-Homburg 1769 - 1829* | Ernst King of Hannover 1771 – 1851 *married Friederike of Mecklenburg-Strelitz 1778 - 1841* |

Victoria Queen of Great Britain 1819 - 1901 *married Albert of Saxe-Coburg 1819 - 1861*

George V King of Hannover *(deposed 1866)* 1819 – 1878 *married Marie of Saxe-Altenburg 1818 - 1907*

Great Britain

Hannover

3. THE DUKES OF MECKLENBURG-SCHWERIN
AND THE BUILDERS OF LUDWIGSLUST

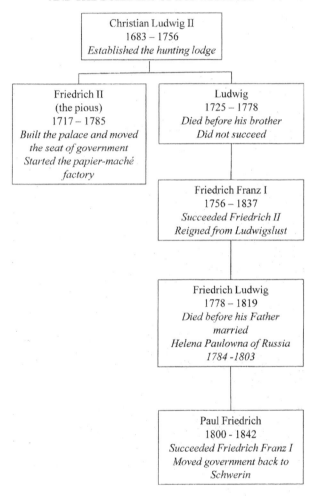

Christian Ludwig II
1683 – 1756
Established the hunting lodge

Friedrich II
(the pious)
1717 – 1785
*Built the palace and moved
the seat of government
Started the papier-maché
factory*

Ludwig
1725 – 1778
*Died before his brother
Did not succeed*

Friedrich Franz I
1756 – 1837
*Succeeded Friedrich II
Reigned from Ludwigslust*

Friedrich Ludwig
1778 – 1819
*Died before his Father
married
Helena Paulowna of Russia
1784 -1803*

Paul Friedrich
1800 - 1842
*Succeeded Friedrich Franz I
Moved government back to
Schwerin*

4. THE LINE OF MECKLENBURG-STRELITZ AND THEIR ROYAL BRIDES

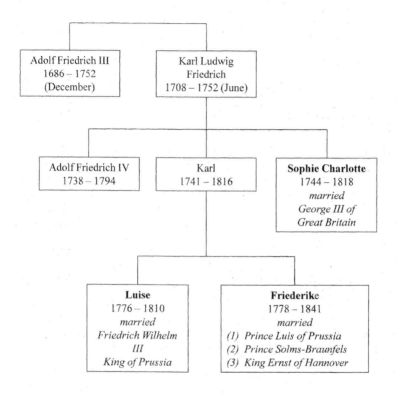

Adolf Friedrich III
1686 – 1752
(December)

Karl Ludwig
Friedrich
1708 – 1752 (June)

Adolf Friedrich IV
1738 – 1794

Karl
1741 – 1816

Sophie Charlotte
1744 – 1818
married
George III of
Great Britain

Luise
1776 – 1810
married
Friedrich Wilhelm
III
King of Prussia

Friederike
1778 – 1841
married
(1) Prince Luis of Prussia
(2) Prince Solms-Braunfels
(3) King Ernst of Hannover

5. THE ANCESTRY OF FREDERICK THE GREAT OF PRUSSIA

Friedrich III Elector of Brandenburg
and later Friedrich I King in Prussia
1657 – 1713
married
Sophie Charlotte of Hannover (Figuelotte)
1668 - 1705

Friedrich Wilhelm I
King in Prussia
1688 – 1740
married
Sophie Dorothee of Hannover
(daughter of Sophie Dorothee of Celle and
George I of Great Britain)
1687 - 1757

Friedrich II
King of Prussia
(Frederick the Great)
1712 - 1786

6. THE DESCENDANTS OF FRIEDRICH WILHELM III AND QUEEN LUISE

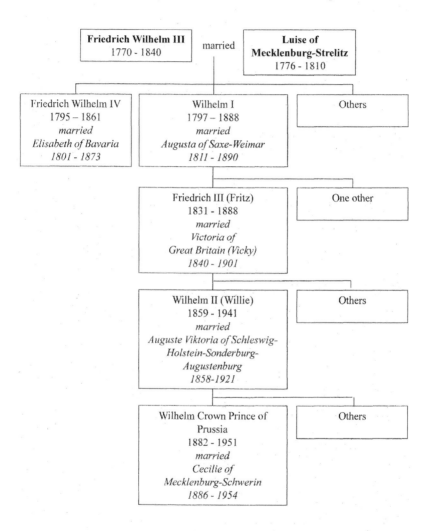

Friedrich Wilhelm III
1770 - 1840

married

**Luise of
Mecklenburg-Strelitz**
1776 - 1810

Friedrich Wilhelm IV
1795 – 1861
married
Elisabeth of Bavaria
1801 - 1873

Wilhelm I
1797 – 1888
married
Augusta of Saxe-Weimar
1811 - 1890

Others

Friedrich III (Fritz)
1831 - 1888
married
Victoria of
Great Britain (Vicky)
1840 - 1901

One other

Wilhelm II (Willie)
1859 - 1941
married
Auguste Viktoria of Schleswig-
Holstein-Sonderburg-
Augustenburg
1858-1921

Others

Wilhelm Crown Prince of
Prussia
1882 - 1951
married
Cecilie of
Mecklenburg-Schwerin
1886 - 1954

Others

7. AUGUSTUS THE STRONG AND COUNTESS COSEL

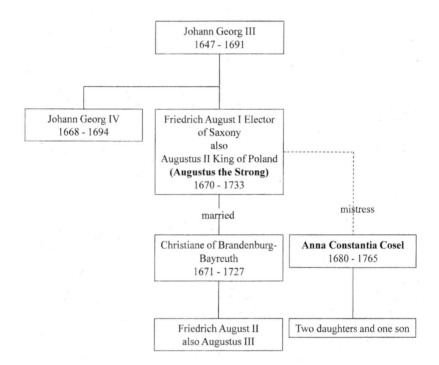

8. THE MARRIAGES OF LUISE, CROWN PRINCESS OF SAXONY

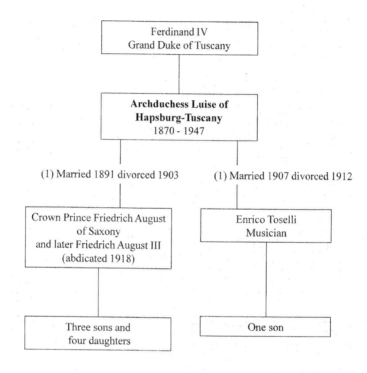

9. THE TWELVE LANDGRAVES OF HESSE-HOMBURG

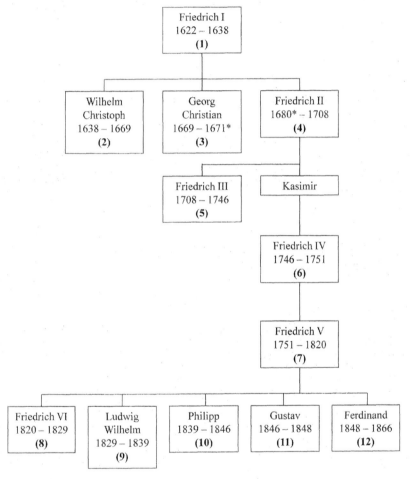

* Chart shows reign dates.

Between the reigns of Georg Christian and Friedrich II, Hesse-Homburg was mortgaged

Appendix C: Timeline to Connect People and Events

1648. The Peace of Westphalia brings an end to the Thirty Years' War, which devastated Europe.

1658. Marriage of Ernst August, Duke of Brunswick-Lüneburg, and Princess Sophia of the Palatine.

1682. Georg Ludwig, the son of Ernst August and Sophia, marries Sophie Dorothee of Celle.

1684. His sister, Sophie Charlotte, marries Elector Friedrich III of Brandenburg.

1692. Ernst August, Duke of Brunswick-Lüneburg, becomes elector of Hannover.

1694. Sophie Dorothee of Celle is divorced and sent to Ahlden for the rest of her life.

1694. Augustus the Strong becomes elector of Saxony.

1701. The Act of Settlement confirms Electress Sophia as heir to the throne of Great Britain.

1701. Elector Friedrich III of Brandenburg is crowned King Friedrich I in Prussia.

1706. Countess Cosel, the mistress of Augustus the Strong, moves into the Tachenbergpalais.

1714. Georg Ludwig of Hannover becomes King George I of Great Britain.

1726. Sophie Dorothee dies at Ahlden.

1740. Frederick the Great succeeds to the throne of Prussia.

1756-1763. The Seven Years' War engulfs much of Europe.

1756. Friedrich II (the Pious) succeeds as duke of Mecklenburg-Schwerin.

1760. George III succeeds as king of Great Britain.

1761. Princess Sophie Charlotte of Mecklenburg-Strelitz marries George III of Great Britain.

1765. Countess Cosel dies at Stolpen after 39 years imprisonment there.

1772.	The divorced Queen Caroline Mathilde of Denmark and Norway arrives in Celle Castle.
1775.	Caroline Mathilde dies at Celle.
1786.	Death of Frederick the Great.
1789.	The storming of the Bastille marks the beginning of the French Revolution.
1789.	George III of Great Britain makes his first visit to Weymouth for the sea bathing.
1793.	Friedrich Franz I of Mecklenburg founds the first German seaside resort at Heiligendamm.
1793.	Luise of Mecklenburg-Strelitz marries the crown prince of Prussia.
1797.	Luise and her husband become king and queen of Prussia.
1803.	Helena Paulowna, Duchess of Mecklenburg-Schwerin, dies.
1803.	The process of secularisation and mediatisation of German states begins.
1806.	Napoleon defeats Friedrich Wilhelm III at the Battles of Jena-Auerstadt and invades Prussia.
1806.	The Holy Roman Empire is dissolved.
1810.	George III is declared insane, and his son becomes regent of Great Britain.
1810.	Death of Queen Luise of Prussia.
1815.	The Emperor Napoleon is finally defeated at the Battle of Waterloo. The Congress of Vienna decides the future of the German states.
1818.	Princess Elizabeth of Great Britain marries Prince Friedrich of Hesse-Homburg.
1820.	Death of King George III of Great Britain. His son becomes George IV.
1837.	Queen Victoria succeeds to the throne. The kingdoms of Great Britain and Hannover are separated; Ernst August I becomes king of Hannover.

1840.   Queen Victoria marries her cousin Albert of Saxe-Coburg-Gotha. Their first child (Vicky) is born nine months later.

1858.   Vicky, Princess Royal of Great Britain, makes her ceremonial entry into Berlin as a new bride.

1859.   Birth of Kaiser Wilhelm II.

1863.   The war of Schleswig-Holstein.

!866.   The Seven Weeks' War; Hannover and other German states are annexed by Prussia.

1870.   Prussia is victorious in the Franco-Prussian War.

1871.   Wilhelm I, King of Prussia, is proclaimed emperor (kaiser) of a new German Empire.

1888.   Kaiser Friedrich III, Vicky's husband, reigns for just 99 days before he dies. His son becomes Kaiser Wilhelm II.

1890.   Wilhelmina succeeds as queen of the Netherlands; Duke Adolf of Nassau becomes grand duke of Luxembourg.

1894.   Vicky moves into her new palace of Friedrichshof.

1899.   The German Castles Association is formed.

1901.   Death of Queen Victoria and, later in the year, of her daughter, Vicky.

1902.   Crown Princess Luise of Saxony runs away from her husband.

1905.   Duchess Cecilie of Mecklenburg-Schwerin marries Crown Prince Wilhelm of Prussia.

1913.   Ernst August III, Duke of Brunswick, marries Princess Viktoria Luise of Prussia.

1914.   World War I begins.

1917.   Crown Princess Cecilie moves into Cecilienhof, the last royal schloss built in Germany.

1918.   World War I ends. Abdication of Kaiser Wilhelm II and the other ruling German princes.

1939.   World War II begins.

1945.   The end of World War II. The Allies set up British, French, US, and Soviet zones in Germany. The Cold War begins.

1949.   Germany becomes two separate countries; the Federal
          Republic of Germany (West) and the German Democratic
          Republic (East).
1954.   Friedrichshof opens as the Schloss Hotel Kronberg.
1961.   The Berlin Wall goes up.
1989.   The Berlin Wall comes down.
1990.   Reunification of East and West Germany.
2001.   The von Stralendorff family buy back Schloss Gamehl at
          auction.

Appendix D: List of Illustrations

Unless otherwise credited, illustrations are from the author's collection.

1. Celle Castle with the unusual gable frontage (courtesy of Residenzmuseum in Celle Castle/Fotostudio Loeper Celle).
2. Duke Georg Wilhelm of Celle and his duchess, Eleonore d'Olbreuse; their romance caused uproar in the family (both portraits courtesy of Residenzmuseum in Celle Castle/Fotostudio Loeper Celle).
3. Sophie Dorothee of Celle with her two children before her divorce (courtesy of Residenzmuseum in Celle Castle/Fotostudio Loeper Celle).
4. Ahlden, where Sophie Dorothee of Celle spent over 30 years under house arrest.
5. Sophia of Hannover in 1648 (from the Historical Museum Hannover courtesy of Herrenhausen Gardens).
6. The garden of Sophia at Herrenhausen, with the new palace in the background.
7. The fairy-tale castle of Marienburg dominates the landscape.
8. The Contrast: print comparing the elderly King Ernst August of Hannover, with the young and popular Queen Victoria (W. Spooner 1830s).
9. King George V of Hannover as a young man; he was always shown in profile to help disguise his disability (print from steel engraving by T.A. Dean after a painting by G.L. Saunders, 1832).
10. The elegant garden front of the Grand Duke's Palace in Bad Doberan.
11. Burg Hohenzollern in the royal sea bathing resort of Heiligendamm.
12. Our favourite schloss—the palace square at Ludwigslust.
13. The mausoleum of Duchess Helena Paulowna, who died before she was out of her teens.
14. Statue of Friedrich Franz I outside the schloss at Ludwigslust.
15. Schloss Schwerin has an amazing position on an island in the lake in the centre of town.

16. Crown Princess Cecilie and her two eldest children (vintage postcard from the Rotary Photographic Series).
17. The schloss at Güstrow was remodelled by Duke Ulrich to rival his brother's at Schwerin (guentermanaus/Shutterstock).
18. The neo-Gothic hunting lodge at Gelbensande, where Cecilie became engaged.
19. The museum and restaurant at Gelbensande.
20. Wiligrad is now an artists' colony and sculpture park.
21. Wiligrad is surrounded by subsidiary buildings.
22. Vicky at the time of her engagement to Prince Friedrich of Prussia (by Richard James after Franz Xaver Winterhalter, 1856).
23. The Altes Palais in Berlin, where Vicky lived as a new bride (print from engraving by A.H. Payne after A. Carse, around 1865).
24. Sanssouci was a favourite home of Frederick the Great (vintage postcard Hans Andres, Berlin-Frohnau).
25. Frederick (centre) in 1741, at the beginning of his reign (engraving after the 1855 painting by Adolf Menzel).
26. The Neues Palais was built to show the wealth and power of Prussia (print from steel engraving by Lemaitre, 1842).
27. The dying Kaiser Friedrich III during his short reign; he died at the Neues Palais (The Illustrated London News, 2 June 1888, from a sketch by E. Hosang).
28. Queen Victoria arrives at Charlottenburg (The Illustrated London News, 5 May 1888, from a sketch by E. Hosang).
29. Charlottenburg was named in honour of Sophie Charlotte, the first queen in Prussia (badahos/Shutterstock).
30. The Two Graces – Queen Luise and her sister, Friederike, who later became queen of Hannover (engraving by Ludwig Schiabonetti after the 1795 painting by Friedrich August Tischbein).
31. The mausoleum of Queen Luise in the schloss garden at Charlottenburg (lithograph from 1840).
32. Schloss Paretz, the favourite home of Friedrich Wilhelm III and Queen Luise.

33. Friedrich Wilhelm III survived his first wife by thirty years – the mausoleum of Queen Luise is shown in the background of his portrait (lithograph showing the king later in life).
34. Cecilienhof is modelled on an English country house (illustration from a report at the time of completion of the schloss).
35. Crown Prince Wilhelm and Crown Princess Cecilie at the start of World War I (vintage postcard, Gustav Liersch, Berlin).
36. World War I was raging when Cecilienhof was built – original sketch of Kaiser Wilhelm II (called *The God of War: Who Never Took Part in a Battle*).
37. The Residenzschloss in Dresden houses the famous Green Vaults.
38. Portrait of Augustus the Strong in the Furstenzug (Procession of Princes).
39. The Taschenbergpalais, from which Crown Princess Luise of Saxony ran away (courtesy of the Taschenbergpalais Hotel).
40. When Luise of Saxony ran away from her husband it caused a sensational scandal that was covered in the international press (the Black and White Budget, 3 January 1903; *The Runaway Royalities: Princess Louise of Saxony has run away from her husband, the Crown Prince, while her brother, the Archduke Leopold Frederick (inset), accompanies her in exile with his own friend, an actress*).
41. The schloss church next to the Taschenbergpalais in Dresden (vintage postcard).
42. Stolpen was a remote Wettin castle when Countess Cosel was imprisoned there (view of the castle and town of Stolpen in 1758 courtesy of Stolpen Castle).
43. Countess Cosel, who tried to blackmail her royal lover after their affair ended (courtesy of Stolpen Castle).
44. Burg Stolpen is built on a dramatic natural feature—an outcrop of basalt.
45. Pillnitz Palace seen from the Elbe River (LianeM/Shutterstock).
46. Pillnitz has a famous collection of plants in pots (vintage postcard Otto Günther, Dresden).

47. The Bergpalais at Pillnitz (vintage postcard).
48. An old postcard shows a view of Colditz castle from the River Mulde (vintage postcard, Louis Glaser, Leipzig).
49. Colditz evokes strong memories of its days as a famous prisoner-of-war camp.
50. The schloss at Rochlitz, in a beautiful spot on a bend in the river (Igor Plotnikov/Shutterstock).
51. Commemorative plaque showing that after World War II, Rochlitz was an interrogation centre for the Soviet secret police.
52. Friedrichshof is a wonderful place to stay for anyone who likes royal history (courtesy of Schloss Hotel Kronberg).
53. Vicky towards the end of her life (print from a photograph by T. A. Voigt, 1900).
54. The writing table in the Kaiser Wilhelm suite is thought to be the original (courtesy of Schloss Hotel Kronberg).
55. The Prince's Garden at Burg Kronberg.
56. Burgruine Königstein was dynamited by French troops in the revolutionary wars.
57. The Luxembourg Palais was a summer residence for the house of Nassau.
58. View of Schloss Bad Homburg from the Schloss Garden, showing the White Tower (courtesy of Schloss Bad Homburg).
59. Princess Elizabeth of Great Britain, who was happy in her new life at Bad Homburg (1798 portrait by William Beechey courtesy of Schloss Bad Homburg).
60. The King's Wing at Schloss Bad Homburg (courtesy of Schloss Bad Homburg).

Appendix E: Map of Germany

This map (which is hand drawn) shows the sixteen federal states of Germany and the approximate location of the 25 schlösser included in this book. Please use the list in the next appendix to match the numbers with the individual schlösser.

Appendix F: Addresses and Website Details for the 25 Schlösser

LOWER SAXONY

1. Schloss Celle
   Schlossplatz 1
   29221 Celle
   www.residenzmuseum.de

2. Schloss Ahlden
   Grosse Strasse 1
   29693 Ahlden
   www.schloss-ahlden.de

3. Herrenhausen gardens
   Herrenhäuserstrasse 4
   30419 Hannover
   www.hannover.de/herrenhausen

4. Schloss Marienburg
   Marienburg 1
   30982 Pattensen
   www.schloss-marienburg.de

MECKLENBURG-POMERANIA

5. Grossherzogliche Palais
   August-Bebel-Strasse
   18209 Bad Doberan

6. Schoss Ludwigslust
   Schlossfreiheit
   19288 Ludwigslust
   www.schloss-ludwigslust.de

7. Schloss Schwerin
   Lennéstrasse 1
   19053 Schwerin
   www.schloss-schwerin.de

8. Schloss Güstrow
   Franz-Parr-Platz 1
   18273 Güstrow
   www.schloss-guestrow.de

9. Jagdschloss Gelbensande
   Am Schloss 1
   18182 Gelbensande
   www.jagdschloss-gelbensande.de

10. Schloss Wiligrad
    Wiligrader Strasse 17
    19069 Lubstorf
    www.mv-schloesser.de

BERLIN AND BRANDENBURG

11. Altes Palais
    Unter den Linden 9
    10117 Berlin
    www.berlin.de

12. Schloss Sanssouci
    Maulbeerallee
    14469 Potsdam
    **www.spsg.de/schloesser-gaerten/
    objekt/schloss-sanssouci**

13. Neues Palais
    Am Neuen Palais
    14469 Potsdam
    www.spsg.de/schloesser-gaerten/
    objekt/neues-palais

14. Schloss Charlottenburg
    Spandauer Damm 10-12
    14059 Berlin
    www.spsg.de/schloesser-gaerten/
    objekt/schloss-charlottenburg

15. Schloss Paretz
    Parkring 1
    14669 Ketzin
    www.spsg.de/schloesser-gaerten/
    objekt/schloss-paretz

16. Schloss Cecilienhof
    Im Neuen Garten 11
    14469 Potsdam
    www.spsg.de/schloesser-gaerten/
    objekt/schloss-cecilienhof

SAXONY

17. Residenzschloss
    Taschenberg 2
    01067 Dresden
    www.schloesserland-sachsen.
    de/schloesser

18. Taschenbergpalais
    Taschenberg 3
    01067 Dresden
    www.kempinski.com/en/
    dresden/hotel-taschenbergpalais

19. Burg Stolpen
    Schlossstrasse 10
    01833
    Stolpen
    www.burg-stolpen.org

20. Schloss Pillnitz
    August-Böckstiegel-Strasse 2
    01326 Dresden
    www.schlosspillnitz.de

21. Schloss Colditz
    Schlossgasse 1
    04680 Colditz
    www.schloss-colditz.com

22. Schloss Rochlitz
    Sörnziger Weg 1
    09306 Rochlitz
    www.schloss-rochlitz.de

HESSE

23. Friedrichshof
    Hainstrasse 25
    61476 Kronberg im Taunus
    www.schloss-hotel-kronberg.de

24. Burgruine Königstein
    Burgweg
    61462 Königstein im Taunus
    www.kur-koenigstein.de

25. Schloss Bad Homburg
    Schlossplatz
    61348 Bad Homburg vor
    der Höhe
    www.schloesser-hessen.de/
    badhomburg

NOTES ON SOURCES

The contents of this book include a mixture of historical information and current-day observations about each of the schlösser included. The current-day observations about each schloss come from my experience of visiting that schloss on a particular day. They are entirely personal; another visitor on a different day could have a different experience.

The historical information comes from two main types of sources. The first of these is the information that was available at each schloss, including the museum displays, guide books if available in English, and the answers from museum attendants, curators, or others to questions. The second type includes the original and secondary sources listed in the bibliography, which I read or reread while writing the book, and my wider knowledge from reading about the history of European royalty over many years.

The following notes give the specific source of direct quotes and certain other historical information included in the text.

1. Sophia, Electress of Hanover. *Memoirs 1630-1680.* (London: Richard Bentley and Son, 1888), 151.
2. Stella Tillyard, *A Royal Affair: George III and his Troublesome Siblings.* (London: Chatto and Windus, 2006), 221.
3. Maria Kroll, *Sophie, Electress of Hanover.* (London: Victor Gollanz.1973),187.
4. Malcolm Balen, A Very English Deceit: The Secret History of the South Sea Bubble and the First Great Financial Scandal. (London: Fourth Estate, 2002), 46.
5. Sophie, *Memoirs 1630-1680,* 68.
6. Hanae Komachi and Henning Queren, *Herrenhausen Gardens.* (Rostock: Hinstorff, 2008), 18.
7. Komachi and Queren, *Herrenhausen Gardens,* 22.
8. Jillian Robertson, *The Royal Race for the British Crown 1817-1819.* (London: Blond and Briggs.1977), Title page.

9. Viktoria Luise, *The Kaiser's Daughter: Memoirs of HRH Victoria Luise, Duchess of Brunswick and Lüneburg, Princess of Prussia*. (London. W H Allen and Co. 1977), 55

10. Heike Kramer, *Palace Ludwigslust*. (Staatliches Museum Schwerin Art Collections, Palaces and Gardens), 40

11. Constance Wright, *Louise, Queen of Prussia*. (London: Frederick Muller, 1970), 14.

12. Cecilie, Ex-Crown Princess of Prussia, *The Memoirs of the Crown Princess Cecilie*. (London: Victor Gollanz, 1931), 32.

13. *Schencks Castles and Gardens: Historic Houses and Heritage Sights*. (Hamburg: Schenck Verlag, 2012).

14. Coryne Hall, 'The Daughter of Grand Duke Michael Nikolaievich: Grand Duchess Anastasia Michaelovna—Grand Duchess of Mecklenburg-Schwerin', *The Grand Duchesses: Daughters and Granddaughters of Russia's Tsars*. (Oakland: EuroHistory.Com, 2004), 80.

15. Hannah Pakula, *An Uncommon Woman: The Empress Frederick*. (London: Weidenfeld and Nicolson, 1996), 90.

16. Christopher Hibbert (Editor), *Queen Victoria in Her Letters and Journals: A Selection by Christopher Hibbert*. (New York: Viking, 1985), 100.

17. Chester Easum, *Prince Henry of Prussia: Brother of Frederick The Great*. (Wisconsin: The University of Wisconsin Press, 1942), 241.

18. Lytton Strachey, *Books and Characters: French and English*. (London: Chatto and Windus, 1922), 159.

19. Strachey, *Books and Characters*, 183.

20. Sir Frederick Ponsonby (Editor), *Letters of The Empress Frederick*. (London: Macmillan and Co, 1928), 326.

21. Rudolf G Sharmann, *Charlottenburg Palace: Royal Prussia in Berlin*. (Munich, Prestel Verlag, 2012), 53.

22. Wright, *Louise, Queen of Prussia*, 18.

23. Wright, *Louise, Queen of Prussia*, 157. Luise is writing to her husband from Konigsberg during the period of political uncertainty following

the defeat at Jena-Auerstadt.

24. John Wardroper, *Wicked Ernest: An Extraordinary Royal Life Revealed.* (London: Shelfmark Books, 2002), 74.

25. Klaus Merten, *German Castles And Palaces.* (London, Thames and Hudson, 1999), 12.

26. Winston Churchill, 'Speech of 5 March 1946 in Fulton, Missouri, USA', *Chronicle of the 20th Century.* (London, Longman, 1988), 640.

27. Iselin Gundermann, *Kronprinzessin Cecilie.* (Karwe: Edition Rieger, 2004), 20.

28. Ex-Crown Princess of Prussia, *The Memoirs of Crown Princess Cecilie,* 244.

29. John Eisenhammer, 'Eggs and Chilly Silence Greet the Queen in Dresden.' *The Independent.* 23 October 1992.

30. Charlotte Zeepvat, 'The Bolter: Archduchess Luisa of Tuscany, Crown Princess of Saxony.' *Royalty Digest Quarterly.* (2010), 36.

31. Luise, Ex-Crown Princess of Saxony, *My Own Story.* (London: Eveleigh Nash, 1911), 180.

32. Greg King and Sue Woolmans, *The Assasination of the Archduke.* (London: Macmillan, 2013), 67-71.

33. Joseph J. Kraszewski, *Memoirs of The Countess Cosel.* (New York: Brentanos, London: Downey and Co Ltd, 1902), 243.

34. Kraszewski, *Memoirs of The Countess Cosel,* 324-329.

35. Catherine Scott-Clark and Adrian Levey, 'Where is the Amber Room?' *The Folio Book of Historical Mysteries.* (London: The Folio Society, 2008), 301.

36. Wikipedia, the free encyclopedia, *States of the German Empire.*

37. Pakula, *An Uncommon Woman,* 590.

38. Flora Fraser, *Princesses: The Six Daughters of George III.* (London: John Murray, 2004), 200.

39. Lucille Iremonger, *Love and the Princess.* (London: Faber and Faber, 1958), 153.

BIBLIOGRAPHY

Balen, Malcolm. *A Very English Deceit: The Secret History of the South Sea Bubble and the First Great Financial Scandal.* London: Fourth Estate, 2002.

Cecilie, Ex-Crown Princess of Prussia. *The Memoirs of the Crown Princess Cecilie.* London: Victor Gollanz, 1931.

Drinkuth, Friederike. *Queen Charlotte: A Princess from Mecklenburg-Strelitz Ascends the Throne of England.* Schwerin: Thomas Helms Verlag, 2011.

Easum, Chester. *Prince Henry of Prussia: Brother of Frederick The Great.* Wisconsin: The University of Wisconsin Press, 1942.

Eggers, Reinhold. *Colditz: The German Story.* Barnsley: Pen and Sword Military, 2007.

Feldhahn, Ulrich. *Prussian Kings and German Kaisers.* Lindenberg: Kunstverlag Josef Fink, 2012.

Flemming, Thomas. *The Berlin Wall: Division of a City.* Berlin; Bebra Verlag, 2011.

Fraser, David. *Frederick the Great: King of Prussia.* London: Allen Lane, 2000.

Fraser, Flora. *Princesses: The Six Daughters of George III.* London: John Murray, 2004.

Fulford, Roger. *Friedrichshof: Home of the Empress Frederick.* Regensburg: Schnell and Steiner, 2002.

Gehrlein, Thomas. *Das Haus Mecklenburg.* Werl: Borde Verlag, 2012.

Guidebooks in English are available at some of the 25 schlösser; they are not separately listed here.

Gunderman, Iselin. *Kronprinzessin Cecilie.* Karwe: Edition Rieger, 2004.

Hall, Coryne. 'The Daughter of Grand Duke Michael Nikolaievich: Grand Duchess Anastasia Michaelovna—Grand Duchess of Mecklenburg-Schwerin', *The Grand Duchesses: Daughters and Granddaughters of Russia's Tsars.* Edited by Arturo E Beéche. Oakland: EuroHistory.Com, 2004.

Helfricht, Jurgen. *Die Wettiner: Sachsens Könige, Herzöge, Kurfürsten, und Markgrafen.* Leipzig: Sachsenbuch, 2012.

Hibbert, Christopher (Editor). *Queen Victoria in Her Letters and Journals:*

A Selection by Christopher Hibbert. New York: Viking, 1985.

Iremonger, Lucille. *Love and the Princess.* London: Faber and Faber, 1958.

King Greg and Woolmans Sue. *The Assassination of the Archduke.* London: Macmillan, 2013.

Komachi, Hanae and Queren, Henning. *Herrenhausen Gardens.* Rostock: Hinstorff, 2008.

Kraszewski, Joseph J. *Memoirs of The Countess Cosel.* New York: Brentanos, London: Downey and Co, 1902.

Kroll, Maria. *Sophie Electress of Hanover.* London: Victor Gollanz, 1973.

Kruger, Renate. *Schwerin Castle: Residence and Monument.* Rostock: Hinstorff, 2004.

Louda, Jîrí and Maclagan, Michael. *Lines of Succession: Heraldry of the Royal Families of Europe.* London: Orbis Publishing, 1981.

Luise, Ex-Crown Princess of Saxony. *My Own Story.* London: Eveleigh Nash, 1911.

Merten Klaus. *German Castles And Palaces.* London: Thames and Hudson, 1999.

Nelson, Walter Henry. *The Soldier Kings.* London: J. M. Dent and Sons, 1971.

Official joint guide of the heritage administrations of several German states. *Time to Travel: Travel in Time to Germany's Finest Stately Homes, Gardens, Castles, Abbeys and Roman Remains.* Regensburg: Schnell and Steiner, 2010.

Pakula, Hannah. *An Uncommon Woman: The Empress Frederick.* London: Weidenfeld and Nicolson, 1996.

Pantenius, Michael. Taschenbergpalais. *From the Palace of Countess Cosel to Grand Hotel.* Halle: Mitteldeutscher Verlag, 2011.

Ponsonby, Sir Frederick (Editor). *Letters of the Empress Frederick.* London: Macmillan and Co, 1928.

Reepen, Iris. *Landgravine Elizabeth, Her Apartments in Schloss Homburg and Her Gardens.* Regensburg: Schnell and Steiner, 2003.

Reid, Pat. *The Colditz Story.* London: Hodder and Stoughton, 1952.

Reiners, Ludwig. *Frederick the Great.* London: Oswald Wolff, 1960.

Robertson, Jillian. *The Royal Race for the British Crown*. London: Blond and Briggs, 1977.

Schencks Castles and Gardens: Historic Houses and Heritage Sights. Hamburg: Schenck Verlag, 2012.

Schnaibel, Marlies. *Luise: Queen of Prussia*. Karwe: Edition Rieger, 2005.

Sharp, Tony. *Pleasure and Ambition: The Life, Loves and Wars of Augustus the Strong 1670-1707*. London: I.B. Taurus, 2001.

Schmidt, Michael. *The Augustan Age and the Dresden Baroque*. Dresden: Sonnenblumen Verlag, 2013.

Sophia, Electress of Hanover. *Memoirs 1630-1680*. London: Richard Bentley and Son, 1888.

Strachey, Lytton. *Books and Characters: French and English*. London: Chatto and Windus, 1922.

Tillyard, Stella. *A Royal Affair: George III and his Troublesome Siblings*. London: Chatto and Windus, 2006.

Ward, Adolphus William. *The Electress Sophia and the Hanoverian Succession*. London: Longmans Green and Co, 1909.

Viktoria Luise, Duchess of Brunswick and Lüneburg. *The Kaiser's daughter: Memoirs of HRH Viktoria Luise, Duchess of Brunswick and Luneburg, Princess of Prussia*. London: W H Allen and Co, 1977.

Wardroper, John. *Wicked Ernest: An Extraordinary Royal Life Revealed*. London: Shelfmark Books, 2002.

Woodham-Smith, Cecil. *Queen Victoria: Her Life and Times 1819-1861*. London: Hamish Hamilton, 1972.

Wright, Constance. *Louise, Queen of Prussia*. London: Frederick Muller, 1970.

Zagolla, Robert. *Saxony: A Short History*. Berlin: Bebra Verlag, 2008.

Zeepvat, Charlotte. 'Prettier than Baden: Royalty and the Spa Town of Bad Homburg', *Royalty Digest: A Journal of Record*, 2002.

Zeepvat, Charlotte. 'Nassau-Weilburg: A Family Album', *Royalty Digest Quarterly*, 2008.

Zeepvat, Charlotte. 'The Bolter: Archduchess Luisa of Tuscany, Crown Princess of Saxony', *Royalty Digest Quarterly*, 2010.

Also published by Roseland Books

Schloss II; More Fascinating Royal History of German Castles
By Susan Symons